LIVING BARNS

How to Find and Restore a Barn of Your Own

LIVING BARNS

How to Find and Restore a Barn of Your Own

Ernest Burden

Bonanza Books
New York

This 1984 edition is published by Bonanza Books, distributed by Crown
Publishers, Inc. by arrangement with Little, Brown and Company.

Manufactured in Hong Kong

Library of Congress Cataloging in Publication Data

Burden, Ernest E., 1934–
  Living barns.

  Bibliography: p.
  Includes index.
    1. Barns—Remodeling.   2. Barns—Conservation
and restoration.   I. Title.
TH3411.B87   1984   690'.89   83-22480
ISBN: 0-517-436175

        h g f e d c b a

Contents

PART ONE BARN COUNTRY   1

1 Barns across America   2
2 Barns as Architecture   18
3 Finding a Barn   26
4 Inside the Barn   34
5 Planning the Conversion   48
6 From Design to Construction   58
7 Commercial Adaptations   74

PART TWO BARNS FOR LIVING   100

8   Barn Homes   102
9   Barns by Architects   114
10 Barn Art   150
11 New Homes from Barn Profiles 166

Bibliography   181
Design Credits   183
Illustration Credits   185
Index   186

PART ONE
Barn Country

Two hundred years ago the United States was a land of farm communities. Today, American farming has largely changed from small family enterprises to a big and specialized business, mechanized to meet the demands of the mass market. Over what was once wilderness and desolate prairie, giant combines harvest wheat; airplanes spray pesticide over acres of corn; and trucks rush cattle, hogs, and milk to crowded cities.

This transformation of American agriculture has left an important structure in its wake — the barn. From the traditional general-use barn of New England to the specialized hop-curing warehouse of California, barns are testimony to a disappearing way of life.

WASHINGTON

OREGON

NEVADA

IDAHO

CALIFORNIA

UTAH

COLORADO

WYOMING

ARIZONA

NEW MEXICO

MONTANA

S. DAKOTA

NEBRASKA

OKLAHOMA

TEXAS

1

2

3

4

By the time the barn was introduced into this country in the early 1700s, it had become a utilitarian shelter for livestock, feed, and tools. It was built to fit its region, climate, and means of cultivation. Faced with a long bitter winter, the early New England farmers devised interconnected barns to avoid venturing outdoors. Similarly, the English who settled in the hot enervating climate of Virginia's Tidewater and who used barns to dry tobacco built comparatively flimsy frames with hinged side boards for ventilation. Between New England and the South lay a region of temperate climate settled by people of diverse cultures. Here the style and customs of the Dutch and the English contributed most to barn building.

The first barns were simply log huts and crude post structures, but with settled farming the neat New England box appeared. On the rich Midwest plains, however, the modest New England barn grew far beyond its original size.

The spreading tidewater tobacco-curing shed and the sturdy Pennsylvania Dutch barn were transplanted

5

6

7

8

10

11

by southern and northern settlers to the western territories. New emigrants from Germany and Scandinavia added to the variety of midwestern styles with new barn forms from peasant Europe. For example, the Scandinavians' barn roofs were steeply pitched to shed snow. Each barn type has its own character.

1. Octagonal barn, California. 2. Log barn with shingled roof, Colorado. 3. Long sweeping roof lines typify California barn. 4. Double-vented hop-curing barn, California. 5. Two barns sharing similar roof lines, Oregon. 6. Pole frame barn and grain silo, California. 7. Weathered gray siding and tin roof, California. 8. Working barns, Illinois. 9. Round barn, Ohio. 10. New England–style connected barn, New Hampshire. 11. Dutch gambrel roof, New Jersey. 12. Decorative cupolas, Pennsylvania. 13. Harvest time, Maryland. 14. Tall silolike barn, North Carolina. 15. Tobacco curing barn, Kentucky. 16. Restored log crib-style barn, Cades Cove, Tenn.

12

13

9

14

15

16

5

Several factors contributed to the distribution of farms across the country. Foremost among these were population, topography, and climate.

The above map depicts graphically the number of dairy cows that existed in 1860, and by interpretation the number of barns that sheltered them. One can see that barns were mostly found in the populated areas of the East, Midwest, and West Coast. With the radical decrease since that time in the number of small working farms, these barns of 100 years ago are rapidly vanishing.

In the Northeast with its abundant forests, the first barns were built of massive timbers, cut with axe and adze. As settlers moved across the country, sawmills were coming into existence so the frames of early midwestern and western barns were made of rough-sawn timbers of smaller dimensions.

The barns of the Midwest were traditional with a difference, since settlement beyond the Appalachians was markedly different from colonial life in the coastal states. New Englanders who migrated to the

plains clung to their old barn shape, but abandoned the continuous connected structures, due to the less severe climate. They also built round and octagonal barns from plans published in farmers' books and journals.

Barns in the Northwest resemble most the working farms of the East, as settlers migrated from New England and the Great Lakes region. Barns in the milder West and Southwest are longer and lower with sweeping roof lines. They are larger in size to accommodate storage of hay for range herds.

1. Newly painted working farm, Washington. 2. Weathered barn, Colorado. 3. Twin silos on northern Oregon barn. 4. Ornamental details adorn California barn. 5. Added-on sheds give this California barn a long roof line. 6. California pole frame barn. 7. New England working farm. 8. Stone end walls and overhanging bay are typical of Pennsylvania barns. 9. Austere Amish barn, southeastern Pennsylvania. 10. Harvest time in Virginia. 11. Curved roof of Pennsylvania barn. 12. Crib-style barn with logs on lower floor.

The barn was introduced into this country by the English and Dutch. Since they colonized the Northeast first, it is natural to find the greatest concentration of their barn styles in this area.

The low, broad Dutch barn is one of the oldest barn types in America. The spread of the roof and the low side walls give this barn its most distinctive appearance. However, by the time many of the Dutch barns were being built, the builders were grandsons of the original settlers. They had no firsthand memories of their European heritage to inspire them and were influenced by their English neighbors. The Dutch barn, in turn, was so widely copied that it became above all others the "standard American barn."

The extraordinary craftsmanship of the Pennsylvania German barns was undoubtedly an American development, since there are no European counterparts. It remained for these German immigrants to combine stone sides and timber cantilevering into a simple but brilliant construction.

The great stone barns of Pennsylvania were possible because of the availability of local limestone, which could be cut easily. In these barns the front wall supports nothing; the entire structure rests on the stone end walls and massive cantilevered timbers of the threshing floor.

At first, barns in the Northeast probably combined living quarters with stables as did their European antecedents. This arrangement with animals and people at opposite ends of a long structure was a pragmatic solution to isolated frontier settlement, where immediate and simultaneous housing of family and livestock was required. Later, the barn was enlarged simply by moving the family out of it. Only after the land was cleared and the barns were built did ordinary settlers turn their attention to homes for themselves.

1. Detail, stone end wall, Bucks County, Pa. 2. Dutch gambrel roof, near Oneonta, N.Y. 3. Large working farm, western Massachusetts. 4. Inscription on barn near Lancaster, Pa. 5. Stone barn, Bucks County, Pa. 6. Classic barn near Allentown, Pa. 7. Large barn and milk shed near Oneonta, N.Y. 8. Decorated barn near Kutztown, Pa.

1

3

5

The tight, convenient, and thrifty New England barn design developed from the rectangular English brick barn, translated into wood for lack of brick. The shape remained unchanged.

Nothing could be simpler or more modest in appearance and plan than this three-bay structure. Used primarily for the storage of crops and hay, it is found all over the Northeast.

One unique feature of the early New England barn is the house as an integral part of the farmstead, i.e., a separate structure, but built adjoining the barn. The connected barn — primarily a series of buildings hooked onto each other without any set pattern or distinguishing feature save expediency — aimed more for convenience of man and beast than for appearance.

Often barns were built on a hillside with one side of the basement wall right up against the hill. If there was any sort of a rise on the farm at all, such a site was invariably chosen. The barn faces south with the barnyard on the sunny side, where in the lee of winter winds cattle can be

8

7

9

turned out on sunny days. The driveway on the north side leading up the rise to the threshing main floor on the second story is the most characteristic feature of the building. These are called "bank barns" to distinguish them from the English type.

Barns in New England vary greatly in the way they are situated on the land, oriented to the weather, and designed. The standards we apply today to some of the best contemporary architecture have their origins in the stylistic individuality of early New England barns.

1. Western Massachusetts. 2. Near Pittsfield, Mass. 3. Octagonal barn and shed, eastern New York. 4. Eastern New York. 5. Large 3-bay English-type barn. 6, 7. In the Berkshires. 8. Northwestern Massachusetts. 9. Western Connecticut, near Roxbury. 10. Western Massachusetts. 11. Southern Vermont.

10

11

6

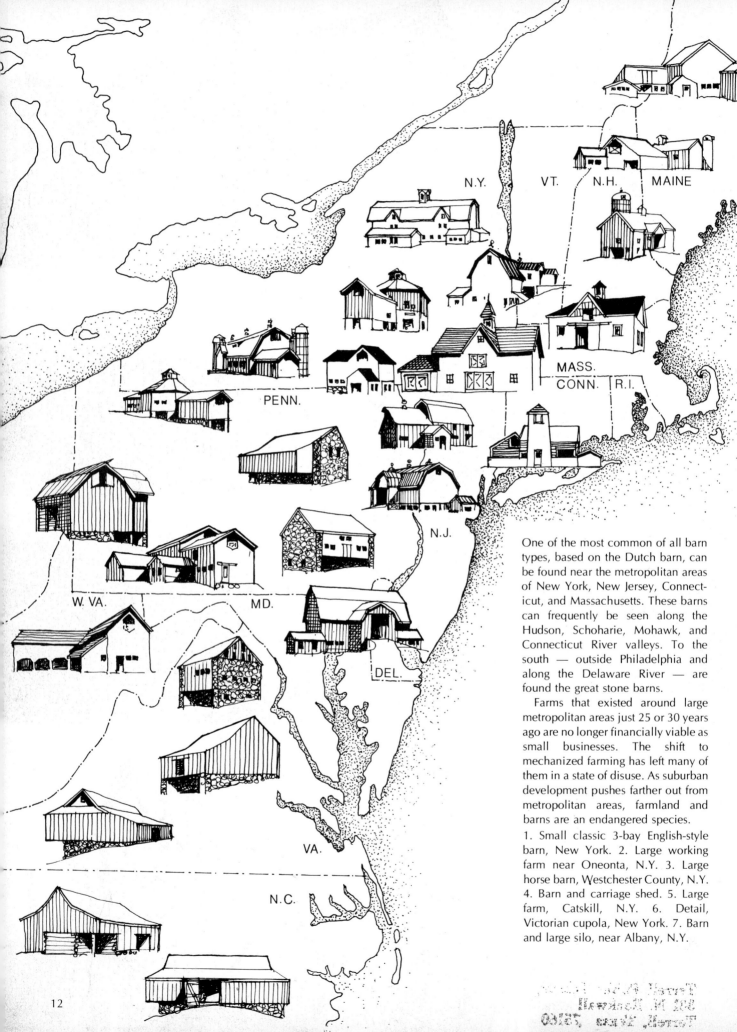

One of the most common of all barn types, based on the Dutch barn, can be found near the metropolitan areas of New York, New Jersey, Connecticut, and Massachusetts. These barns can frequently be seen along the Hudson, Schoharie, Mohawk, and Connecticut River valleys. To the south — outside Philadelphia and along the Delaware River — are found the great stone barns.

Farms that existed around large metropolitan areas just 25 or 30 years ago are no longer financially viable as small businesses. The shift to mechanized farming has left many of them in a state of disuse. As suburban development pushes farther out from metropolitan areas, farmland and barns are an endangered species.

1. Small classic 3-bay English-style barn, New York. 2. Large working farm near Oneonta, N.Y. 3. Large horse barn, Westchester County, N.Y. 4. Barn and carriage shed. 5. Large farm, Catskill, N.Y. 6. Detail, Victorian cupola, New York. 7. Barn and large silo, near Albany, N.Y.

N.Y.   VT.   N.H.   MAINE

MASS.
CONN.   R.I.

PENN.

N.J.

W. VA.   MD.

DEL.

VA.

N.C.

1

2

3

4

5

6

7

* LOCATION
OF BARNS

Barns seem to be everywhere. Or so it appears until you try to find one for yourself. Numerous existing barns are still being used for full-scale or limited farming. It is possible, however, to find barns that are unused, and many that are abandoned.

Although state agriculture departments publish maps of viable farmland, you will not find many unused barns in the listed areas. You need to look in places that were farm communities a generation or two ago, but that are no longer engaged in agriculture.

You might start with an ordinary state road map to choose the rural boundaries within which you will search. Geodetic survey maps are also handy because of their detail. On some maps barns are shown as hollow squares and other buildings as solid shapes.

Do your reconnaissance by map

first, marking all the barns on back roads. Since the roads that now link most major cities were built within the last 20 years, they are unlikely to pass near many barns. Therefore, plan to travel the older back roads if you want to have any luck. Once you leave the main highways, county maps are your best bet since they show sufficient detail to enable you to explore many roads you might otherwise miss.

Try dead ends. They will most likely have a farm at the end, or even several along the way. Look especially for a barn located across the road from a farmhouse, or out in a field. An owner would be more apt to sell that one than a barn next to his house.

All the barns on these pages were found on the county roads shown on the map above, near the town of Jewett, N.Y.

In the East and Midwest the best time to look for barns is in early winter or early spring when there are no leaves on the trees. Although summer and fall driving is more pleasant, it's not practical for barn-hunting.

These aerial photos of a piece of rural property show the summer and winter foliage (2, 3), with corresponding summer and winter views of the barn on that property (4, 5).

If you look in the summer, you may miss over half the barns because they are off the road and hidden from full view. If you are searching for an unused barn in winter, you can look for unplowed driveways and other signs of non-use.

1. Aerial photo of a portion of a farm community in Schoharie, N.Y. 2, 3. Aerial views of property, summer and winter. 4, 5. Summer and winter views of the same barn in the Catskills, N.Y. 6. Hidden barn, New York. 7, 8. Summer and winter views of the same barn near Oneonta, N.Y. 9. Partially hidden barn near Albany, N.Y.

6

7

8

9

CHAPTER 2
Barns as Architecture

As you look for a barn, you will note that domestic housing from early colonial America is closely derived from the local architecture of the settlers' homelands. The homes of our ancestors follow an unbroken pattern of stylistic tradition.

The American barn, on the other hand, shows a variety and yet simple unity of form which have no direct precedent, either in Europe or elsewhere. For this reason it has always been admired by architects as a forthright expression of form developing out of a utilitarian function.

Many have commented on the wonder of barns as examples of architecture without "architects." This view often depicts the builders of barns as lacking concern for their appearance. Barns are, in fact, some of the most truly distinctive indigenous architectural forms in the country. The contemporaneous development of the farmhouse did not exhibit such variety of shape and form, overall experimentation, and unique architectural treatment as the barn. One reason for this individual expression may stem from the complexity of the structure required to enclose such a vast space. Many barns exhibit a stylistic treatment that goes beyond merely echoing the patterns of beams and braces, one that ranks with the most carefully studied pieces of domestic architecture.

The Victorians did not ignore the barn. With a final flurry of Gothic, some barns recall the character of a cathedral, with their arched ceilings and bell towers or cupolas. This is not surprising, since barn and church forms seem to be inextricably min-

1

2

3

4

5

gled in their early development. The three-bay English barn is derived directly from medieval church plans. In some barns one has the same feeling of space and expanse that can be experienced in a cathedral with its arched, soaring roof, and it is easy to relate their origins.

1. Voorhees Castle, Bement, Ill. The structure, with its 68-foot clock tower, was recently destroyed in a tornado. 2. Brickwork openings for ventilation, near Lancaster, Pa. 3. Dormers, shutters, and handmade hardware on a Pennsylvania barn. 4. Round hex signs, painted over the siding, are used as ornamental devices throughout southeastern Pennsylvania. 5. A classically elegant barn, New York. 6. High pointed Gothic windows recall a cathedral, southern Pennsylvania. 7. Small barn, central New York. 8. Ornate cupola, dormers. 9. Classic Victorian carriage house, southwestern Connecticut. 10. Ornamental woodwork on cupola and eaves, central New York.

6

7

8

9

10

Simplicity, symmetry, and balance are but a few of the elements that classify some barns as architecture. To this one can add a willingness on the part of the builder to use forms and relate masses unlike those of any dwelling of the time. Barns often have several shed elements attached to the main mass, and either by design or by accident they relate in a complementary way to the whole in appearance. Other barns display unusual cupolas, or elaborate window designs.

1

2

3

4

5

6

1. Barn and sheds, Lexington, N.Y. 2. Round barn, Champaign, Ill. 3. Snub-nose roof, central Illinois. 4. Restored log crib barn, Tennessee. 5. Middleburg, N.Y. 6. In the Catskills. 7. Windmill-style barn complex, Long Island. 8. Near Lancaster, Pa. 9. Brick and stone barn, Bucks County, Pa. 10. Abstract shapes in barn near Hunter, N.Y.

7

8

9

10

On many farmsteads the barn, out-buildings, and house are all executed in the same architectural style. In these instances it is generally the barn, not the house, that remains architecturally the most impressive.

Barns were not intended as residences, or to be adapted for other human uses. The fact remains, however, that many people have successfully converted barns into dwellings or commercial structures.

Therefore, the barn has a new useful purpose. It is a structure that through adaptive renovation can be made habitable for people. There is a great intrinsic value in being able to preserve and re-use so much space.

Once you have decided on a barn as an alternative to a conventionally

1

2

3

4

built home, you will realize that not every barn is a masterpiece of architecture. In fact, quite the opposite is true. Therefore, when you look for a barn, expect the unexpected.

1. Octagonal barn, upstate New York. 2. Victorian house and barn, lower Catskills, New York. 3. Barn and silo with ornamental vent. 4, 5. Two views of a "home-made" barn with added on sheds and silo, northeastern Pennsylvania. 6. English-style barn near Albany, N.Y. 7. Narrow ventilating slots give a fortresslike appearance to this barn near Lancaster, Pa. 8. Old weathered barn, Catskill Mountains, New York.

6

5

7

8

CHAPTER 3
Finding a Barn

The barn you are apt to find will likely have been unused for years. It may not look inviting from the outside — in fact, it may even be foreboding. It will probably be without a foundation and there will be boards missing and holes in the roof. In short, don't go looking for a dream barn to move into. But once inside you will discover what all other barn-owners love — all that space.

1

When you are looking for a barn, try to get firsthand information from local residents about farms in the area. Also ask the town clerk or local agricultural agents.

Realtors can be helpful, but they will probably show you only what is listed. Chances are your best buys won't even be on the market. Certain land sale agencies advertise widely in most newspaper classified· sections. They deal in nationwide land sales and publish periodic free catalogues. Some list entire farm properties for sale.

Once you have located a barn, check the property deed at the local town hall to verify ownership and to ascertain that the property is free from errors in survey or from deed restrictions. You may want to hire an attorney to check title to the property; some states will require that an attorney does this.

Unless your optimism is well founded and you can talk the owner into a deferred payment scheme, you must be prepared to purchase the barn outright rather than through

2

3

28

4

conventional financing. Few banks will lend money to buy an empty barn and a few acres of land even if you can make a substantial down payment. However, if there are improvements on the property, such as a working sewer or a well, your chances of arranging a loan are better. Of course, there must be electrical service nearby to operate a pump for the well. (Don't assume that a piece of property has a sewer or a well. Many old sewers may no longer work, depending on the absorption quality of the soil. Although barns are often located near streams or springs, this does not guarantee the availability of pure water on the property.) If you are lucky, on the same land will be a farmhouse that has some value, and in this case you are certainly in a better position to qualify for a loan.

1. Near Oneonta, N.Y. 2. Near Cooperstown, N.Y. 3. Connecticut. 4. Western Massachusetts. 5. New Hampshire. 6. Near Kent, Conn. 7. Lexington, N.Y. 8. Near Canaan, Conn.

1

If the barn you find is abandoned, you are in for a lot of work before you can even begin to consider renovation. The first step is to find out who owns the property. If the land is not posted with the owner's or a realtor's name, you can go to the town hall and check the property tax maps for the name and address of the owner. It is also very possible that you can glean information about the property from neighbors.

If the entire farm is truly abandoned, chances are the owner will live in another city altogether. If you are sincerely interested in the barn, pursue the search for the owner. At least you know that the property is inactive and your chances for a bargain price are greater than if it were an active farm.

The abandoned state will mean more damage from the elements or from vandalism, and you will have to examine the value of the structure very carefully. At this point, you may be wise to hire a consulting engineer or contractor, or at least get a builder's opinion on the expenses involved in the project.

2

3

4

5

If you are buying a barn to move to another site, the price is anyone's guess. It can range from a few hundred to a few thousand dollars. Some farmers have given away their barns, and, believe it or not, in exceptional cases some have even paid for them to be taken down and the land cleaned up.

1. Near Fredericksburg, Va. 2. Middletown, N.Y. 3. Near New Milford, Conn. 4. Middleburg, N.Y. 5. Port Jervis, N.Y. 6. Lexington, N.Y. 7. Durham, N.Y. 8. Hunter, N.Y.

7

6

8

31

The discovery of a barn frame indicates that the property or use of the barn has been abandoned for some time. You should consider purchasing frames, however, because in a conversion any extra hand-hewn members can come in handy. Complete frames are quite valuable, and even partial frames that are standing are salvageable and usable as repair or replacement timbers. Once a frame is exposed to the weather, however, it is only a matter of time until it is on the ground. Water will get into the joints and cause rot, then collapse.

Many barns were constructed from more than one set of matching hand-hewn timbers. It is not uncommon to find old barns made from even older barns. It seems quite natural to continue this practice, and many people successfully use parts of several barns in their conversions.

4

6

1. Near Allentown, Pa. 2. Durham, N.Y. 3. Tannersville, N.Y. 4. Near Catskill, N.Y. 5. Richfield Springs, N.Y. 6, 7. Sharon, N.Y. 8. Windham, N.Y.

5

7

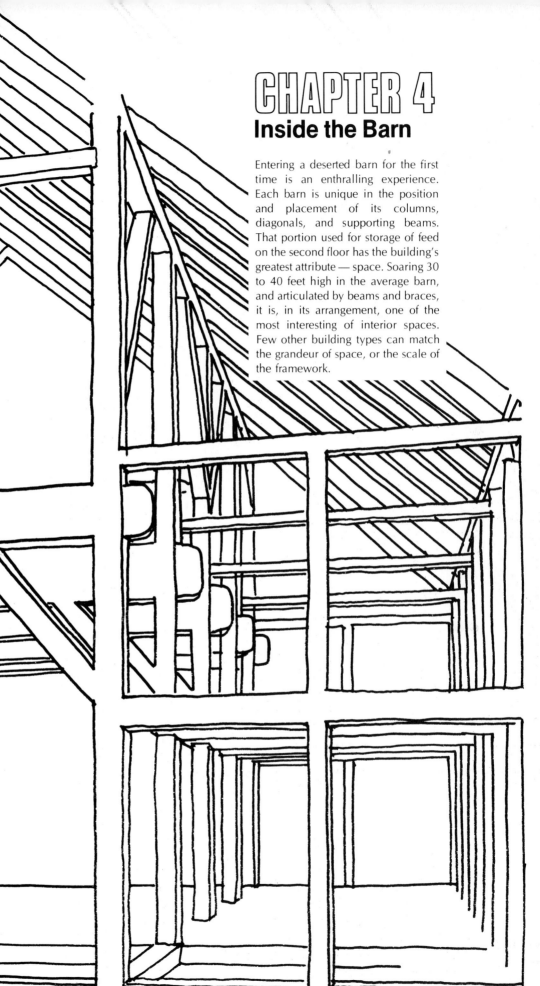

CHAPTER 4
Inside the Barn

Entering a deserted barn for the first time is an enthralling experience. Each barn is unique in the position and placement of its columns, diagonals, and supporting beams. That portion used for storage of feed on the second floor has the building's greatest attribute — space. Soaring 30 to 40 feet high in the average barn, and articulated by beams and braces, it is, in its arrangement, one of the most interesting of interior spaces. Few other building types can match the grandeur of space, or the scale of the framework.

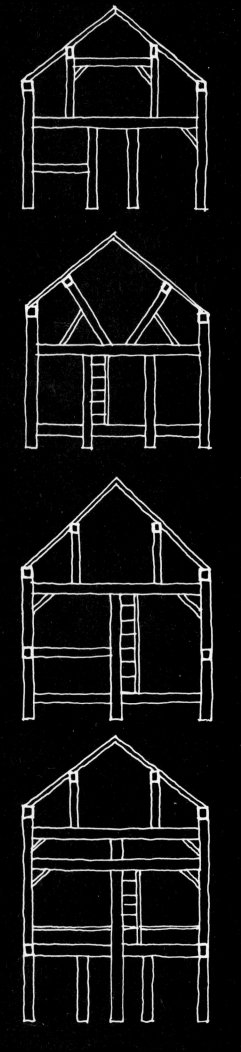

Barns are of noble proportions on the exterior. Their sturdy external appearance, however, gives little hint of the intricate framework within.

One hears much these days about revealed structure in architecture and about the visual quality and expressiveness of interior space. With respect to both of these considerations, the barn is unusually distinguished.

Inside, the entire structural frame is exposed to view. Almost all other building types hide the internal components beneath plaster or paneling, wainscoting or hung ceilings. One rarely gets a chance to see these structural members except when a building is being erected or taken down.

The interior of a barn is very impressive as ordered space. The framing members are ordered and clearly

differentiated, which visually organizes and subdivides the space. The expansive scale is further heightened by the uneven light, which filters through cracks into the virtually windowless interior.

1. Bents of interior framing. 2. Stone Ridge, N.Y. 3. Near Kingston, N.Y. 4. Near Allentown, Pa. 5. Near Lancaster, Pa.

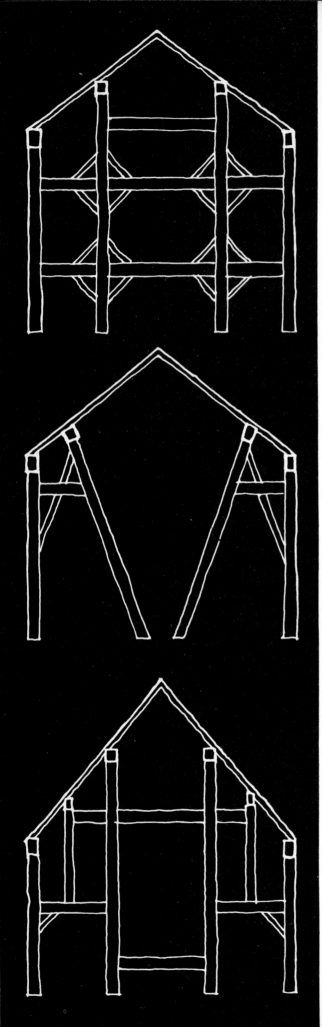

Once inside you may find hazardous conditions. Chances are the interior will be dim. If you are in an abandoned barn and do not have permission to enter, you should exercise caution. The floorboards may have rotted through and collapse when you step on them. Most floors on which hay was stored were covered with thin boards and were not kept up. If possible, walk only where you know there are beams underneath, such as around the perimeter wall or on the center span.

In checking the barn over for structural soundness, look first at the pegged joints. If they are intact and not split, chances are they can be sal-

vaged. Most destruction occurs when water enters through the roof or elsewhere. Whenever the roof is bad, you can be assured of further damage somewhere.

1. Bents of interior framing. 2. Near Fredericksburg, Va. 3. Jewett, N.Y. 4. Near Reading, Pa. 5. Near Fredericksburg, Va.

The strongest parts of any barn are the large timbers and diagonal braces. The weakest parts are the roof and interior floors. If the barn is around 100 years old, the foundation and lower beams will also probably need major repairs or complete replacement. The main threshing floor will generally be sound, since it is usually made of 2-inch-thick boards. It supported teams of horses and in later years tractors and hay wagons.

The floor of the lower level, where the cattle and horses were kept, will usually be in very poor condition, especially in older barns. Sometimes this area will have a poorly maintained wood floor but most often it is

2

4

dirt. This part will need the most extensive cleanup.

Exterior composition varies from weathered gray vertical siding to horizontal siding layered with paint. If the siding is vertical, you will not find interior vertical studs between the massive beams. If the siding is horizontal, rough-sawn studs, usually measuring 2 by 4 inches will be exposed on the inside.

Even if the original siding is in questionable condition, it can serve as interior paneling. It should be taken down carefully, so as not to split the old brittle wood.

An original roof of slate or shingle can be salvaged, but only by an ex-

pert. Because the most expeditious, functional, and inexpensive roofing material for barns is sheet metal, many barns have had their original roof replaced with tin. This can be left on if you wish, but if removed, it cannot be re-used.

Inside the dark barn it may be difficult to envision the full potential of the completed renovated space. But remember that all "living barns" started from these same dark beginnings.

1. Jewett, N.Y. 2. Cobleskill, N.Y. 3. Near Cooperstown, N.Y. 4. Near Allentown, Pa. 5. Any barn, Anywhere, U.S.A.

3

5

The barn you find and want to have for your own may be too close to the road or too close to the farmhouse, or on the wrong lot. If you purchase the barn separately, intending to move it to another site, you will have to make careful plans. Moving or taking apart a barn is no job for a novice, and you will need expert help.

There are several ways of moving a barn. If the move is only a few hundred feet, moving it intact is the quickest way. Most barns rest merely by gravity on a stone foundation because there is no way to fasten the wood sill to the rock foundation. Therefore, it is relatively simple to raise the entire frame using house jacks at key points (1). It may be necessary to use long beams under the lower floor beams to distribute the load equally (2). This is referred to as underpinning. Once the barn is raised and a portion of the foundation is removed for passage of the underpinning, the barn can be pulled by a bulldozer (3). Round logs can be used to facilitate the movement of the barn along a predetermined path.

If you are moving a frame that is particularly fragile, it is a good idea to nail plywood to the frame to strengthen it and keep it from warping. Since all barn beams are pegged, there is a good deal of play in the joints and they can move and even twist to some degree without coming apart.

Taking a frame apart instead of moving it intact can be as much work — if not more — as erecting it in the first place. First, all the members must be carefully identified, and their location noted (4, 5). Any logical identification system can be used; compass points plus an alphabetical or numerical sequence work well. Labels must be applied and related to a prearranged scheme for re-erection. The system for recording the structure should be foolproof. Chalk marks on the beams will rub off. Labels can be lost, torn off, or can simply rust away if the frame is not to be re-erected immediately. Indelible marker on wide masking tape is a fairly good system.

To prevent the frame from collapsing as you dissemble it, you will need to brace it temporarily with 2-by-4s

5

6

(6, 7). Much care must be taken not to destroy the joints. The wooden pegs must be carefully removed by pounding them out backward. When taking apart a barn with large beams a crane will come in handy to lower them to the ground.

7

1

2

3

4

5

44

6

7

After writer-explorer Peter Beard found this windmill (1), he decided to move it in sections to a new site several miles farther out on the tip of Long Island. The buildings consisted of the old mill, house, and shed. Each part of the complex was jacked up, and framing and underpinning were installed for the move (2).

The main mill tower was carried on one truck (3), while the truncated top was carried on another (4). Due to the height of the tower, there were many obstacles along the way, such as overhead wires, traffic signals, and low trees (6, 7). When the buildings finally arrived on the site, they were lowered onto new foundations (8) and reassembled by "cribbing" and the use of house jacks. On part of the new site, extensive work was done to the sea wall to prevent further erosion of the oceanside cliffs (5, 9).

8

9

1

2

3

4

As we have seen, the framework of a barn can be moved by other methods than hauling it intact from one place to another. Richard Babcock, of Hancock, Mass., has been doing just that for 20 years (1). It is a trade he learned from his grandfather, who had a construction business in Williamstown, Mass., where he worked with barn frames and restored many old houses.

Babcock took down his first barn using only a gin pole. He marked each piece and loaded the pieces on a truck to be re-erected miles away by the same method of gin pole and pulleys.

5

6

7

8

9

Since then he has taken down more than two dozen barns, moving them to many different sites. The only barns that appeal to him are the oldest pre-revolutionary Dutch barns. He knows how to find them, having studied how the Dutch settlers made their way up navigable rivers. He even searches early land maps for the names of Dutch farmers.

As Babcock's old methods of dismantling barns gave way, he had a crane built to his own specifications (2). It can be driven off the road and into a field to make the barn more accessible. Its very precise controls allow him to lift beams and rafters carefully out of place. While the crane delicately holds a beam in balance, he drives out the wooden pegs (3) and pries the joints apart (4, 5).

Babcock not only takes the beams, but he takes the slate roof if it is salvageable, and he takes all the stone from the foundation, which he re-uses in fireplaces or stone walls around the perimeter.

On the new site he has a concrete foundation built to the barn's dimensions. Then he brings his crane to the site and begins to re-erect the carefully coded pieces (6, 7). He is continually amazed at how easily they go back together, but he admits that the early barn-builders' unique system of coding by shallow ax-cuts makes it easier to keep track of which brace goes with which beam.

Most owners want to preserve the look of the original barn, and this is precisely what Babcock does. First, he restores the frame, intact, in its original configuration. Then he proceeds to work on the barn from the outside of the beam structure. Once the frame is up and braced he puts on the roof to protect the interior members. Then he puts on, as interior finish, sheetrock, paneling, or the original barn siding. This completely seals the whole frame. Next, he wraps the entire exterior in polyethylene and insulates it. Finally, the exterior siding goes on (8) and windows are cut in as desired. The end result is an interior (9) that began as a faithfully restored barn frame — one that has been saved from the ravages of the elements or from the ever-encroaching bulldozer, and one that Babcock has given his own stamp.

47

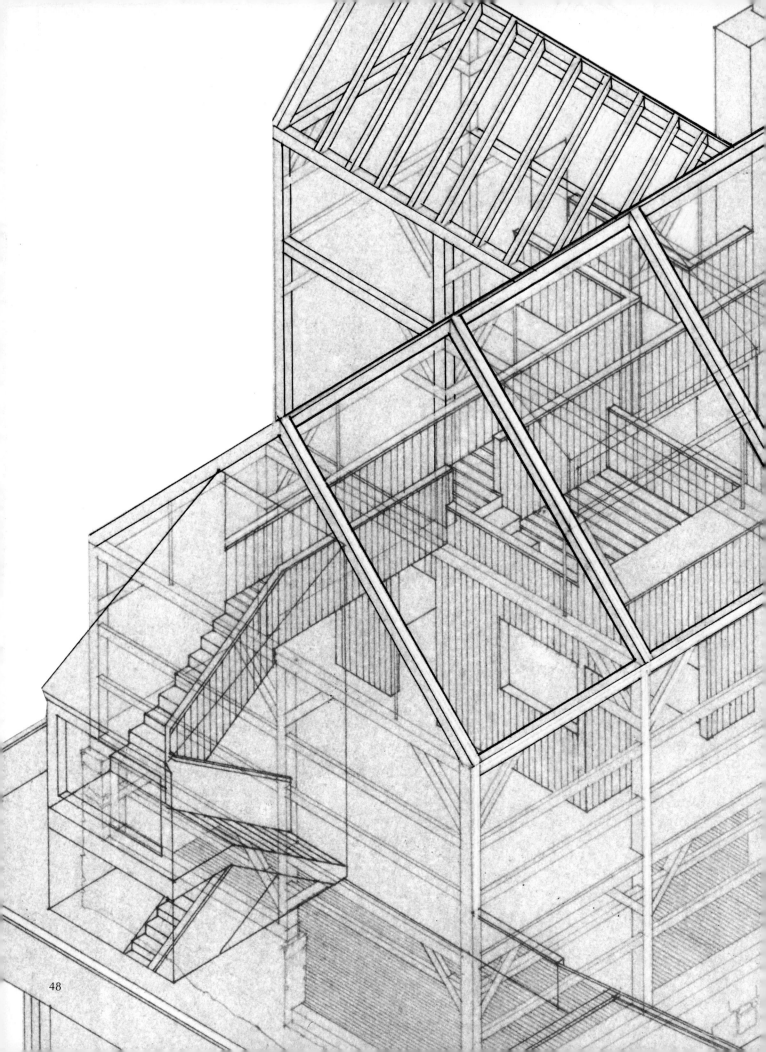

CHAPTER 5
Planning the Conversion

Barn frames and barn spaces are very different from other structures. Except for the few uprights and supporting beams, there are no interior bearing partitions. This tremendous, flexible space can give rise to many imaginative solutions. To actually effect them, however, requires that every design start with rough sketches, study models, design plans, and elevations. It is from these studies, a selection of which follows, that the space is organized and uses arranged according to a pattern for living and/or working.

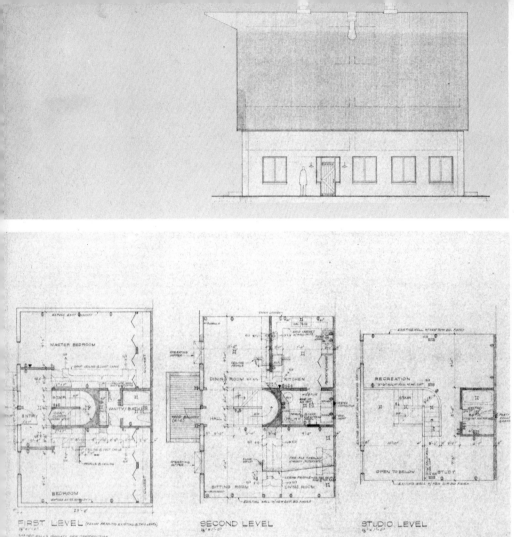

1

2

FIRST LEVEL (PLANS FROM EXISTING 2ND LEVEL)

MASTER BEDROOM

STAIR

VANITY/BATH

ENTRY

BEDROOM

UNITS 2 & 3 (PHASE 2)

SECOND LEVEL

DINING ROOM

HALL

KITCHEN

SITTING ROOM

LIVING ROOM

STUDIO LEVEL

RECREATION

STAIR

OPEN TO BELOW

STUDY

3

This 1930 dairy barn was abandoned over 30 years ago, and the surrounding pastureland in Cary, N.C., was subdivided and developed for residential use. Architect Bill Britt decided to adapt the barn for a home and studio.

Britt intends to restore the exterior to preserve the spirit of the dairy-farming heritage of the area. The interior will be modified into a three-level structure incorporating a loft-type studio for himself and plenty of room for his family.

He began his design studies by first drawing the existing exterior elevations, over which he sketched the new windows (1, 2). He kept the existing roof and ventilating cupolas intact. He developed a revised plan for each of the three floor levels (3), and built a large stairway connecting each level. Then he drew two cross sections through the middle of the building to study the interior spaces in more detail (4, 5).

These preliminary studies indicate the great flexibility of working with a large spatial volume.

5

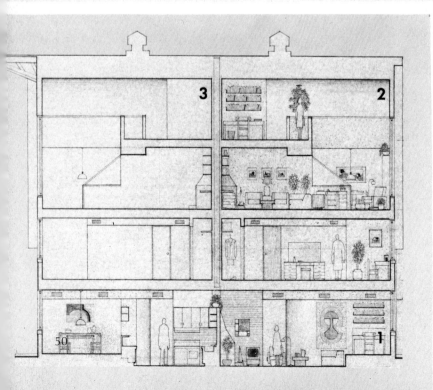

3

2

50

1

4

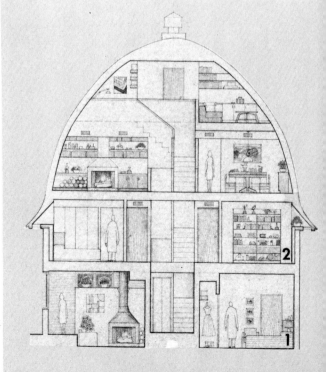

2

1

This project (1) in Franklin, Tenn., is located in the center of a site between a new house designed by another architect and now under construction, and a second existing barn.

The barn will be used as a combination pool house, office, and game room. Architect Frank Orr has proposed a design that does not alter the basic pole frame style. The key design feature of the site is that all three structures have pronounced roof ridge lines (2), which are parallel to each other.

Here the architect has used preliminary sketch plans (3) and a sketch perspective (4) to indicate his design, taking one of the site pictures as the basis for his sketch. The main exterior change in the overall barn form occurs at the entrance. The roof lines remain unaltered.

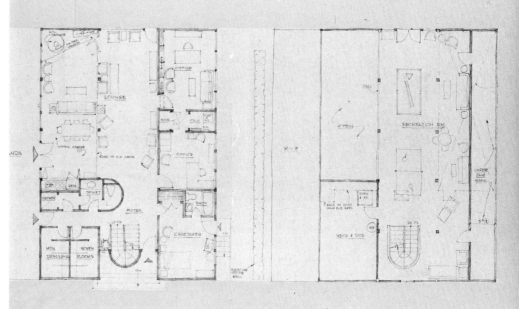

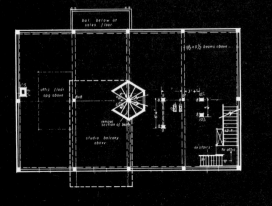

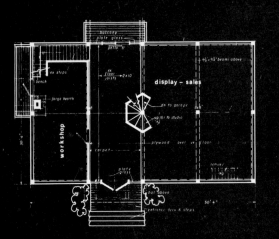

Located on ten acres of land west of Madison, Wis., this feed mill (2) was in need of repair when landscape architect Homer Fieldhouse decided to convert it into office and display space (4). It is of post-and-beam construction, and much of the openness of the existing space was retained.

The intent is to leave the beam structure exposed and to fill in between with stone (3), thereby accenting the skeletal frame. The design was planned around the existing hexagonal stairwell, which is the focal point of the preliminary plans (1).

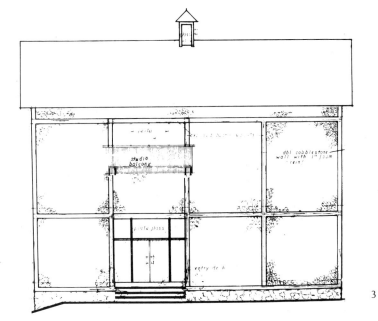

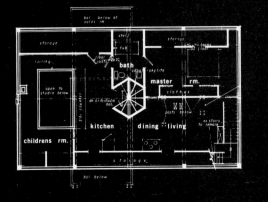

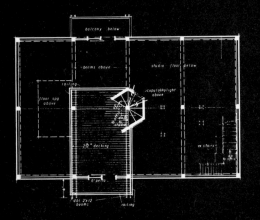

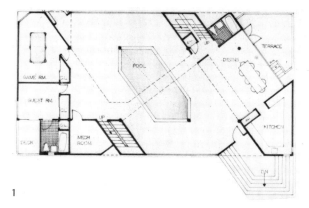

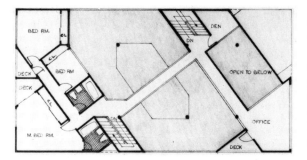

1

2

When architect Peter Hoftyzer purchased this barn in Otsego County, N.Y., he could learn little about its history. However, the mortise-and-tenon joints dated it as pre–World War I.

In his design Hoftyzer kept the frame intact but placed walls diagonally in the plan to create an alternate flow of space within the rectangular structure. The exterior was treated with simple openings.

The architect used plan and elevation studies to make his design apparent (1–3). A teacher of architecture, he used the drawings more as a study for himself than for formal presentation.

He developed a sophisticated treatment for the exterior, using pencil-rendered elevations to study their relation to the plan. Finally, two elevational views were combined into three-dimensional perspective drawings (4).

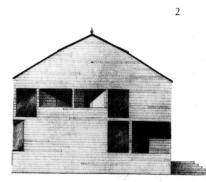

3

4

Study models are very helpful in the design process, especially if they can show interior detail. This barn (1, 2) in Brewster, N.Y., was redesigned by architect David Glasser. His model, made of balsa wood, was constructed to show the interior beams and braces (3, 4). This allowed him to study the structure of the interior in relation to the exterior treatment. The T configuration is a challenging and interesting variation from the standard three-bay rectangle.

1

2

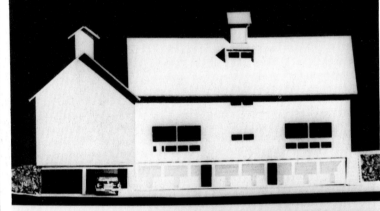

3

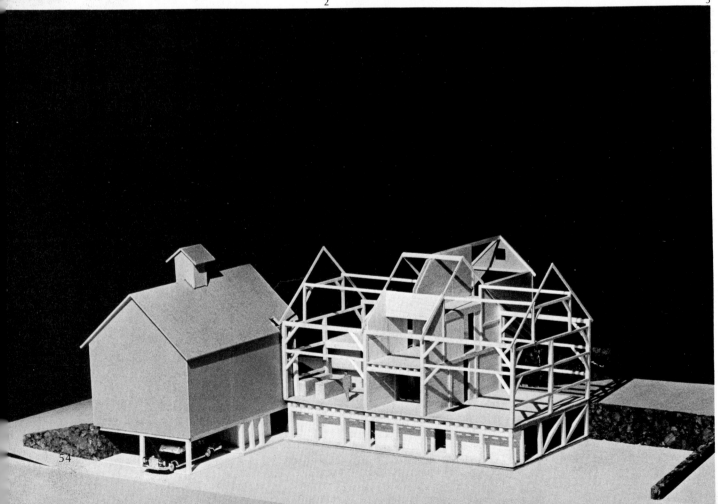

4

Another effective method of studying an interior design is by means of an isometric drawing (4). It resembles a skeletal model in that it shows the relationship between structure and interior function.

In this northwestern Massachusetts barn project, architects Juster Pope Associates designed an upper-level gallery connecting several open bedroom areas. The skeletal drawing clearly shows the platform balconies and interconnecting stairways in relation to the existing structural frame. The architects also utilized a cardboard model (1–3).

1

2

3

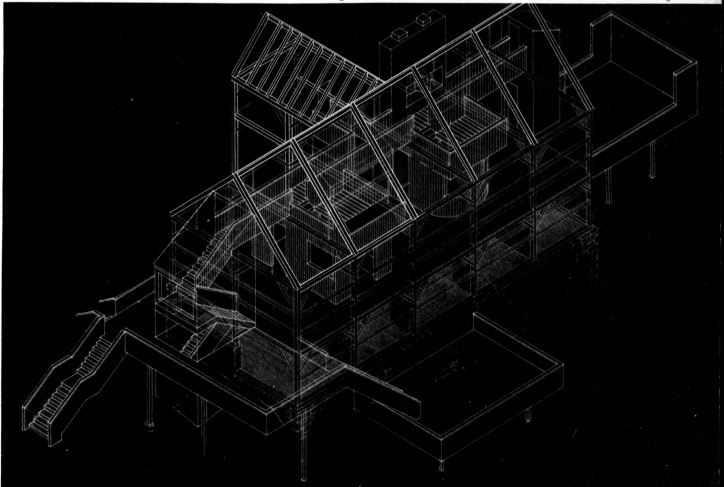

4

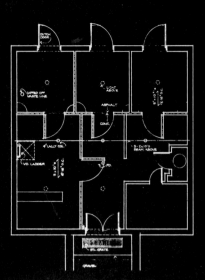
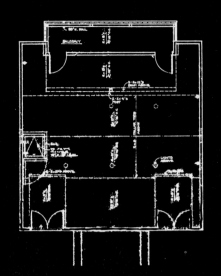
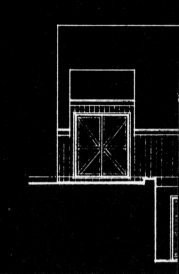

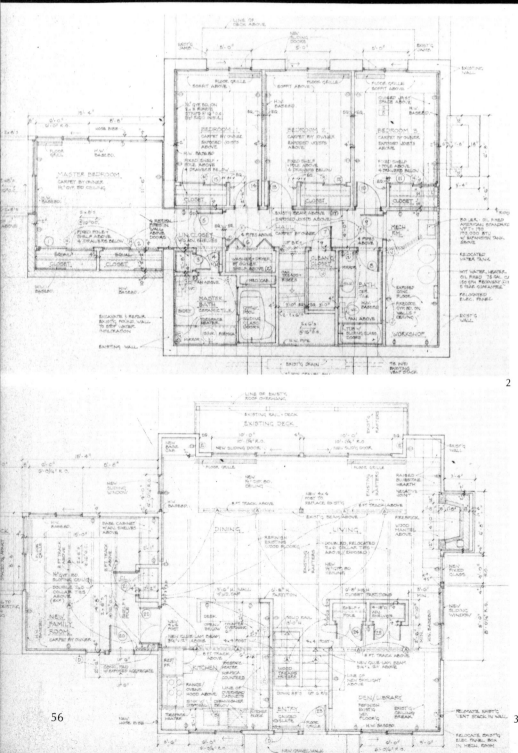

On a small piece of property one of the oldest barns in New Canaan, Conn., has been converted into a dwelling by architect Howard Patterson, Jr. (6–8). He liked the symmetry of the small barn and worked within the existing frame, except for a small addition to one side which has a family room on the lower level and master bedroom above. In the original barn, the entire lower floor was laid up in stone and this was retained in the final design. The rather unusual existing balcony, which projected over the lower doors, was also kept.

The methods used to study the existing barn and the conversion

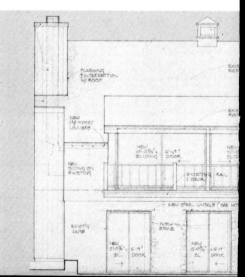

2

3

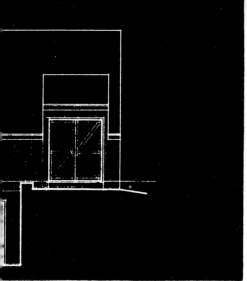

1

6

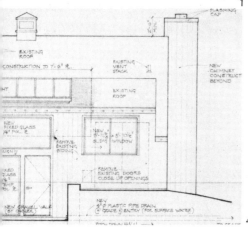

4

were the architect's scaled working plans and elevations (1–5). Both floor levels and all four exterior sides were drawn to the same scale. By studying the "before" drawings, the building contractor could understand and evaluate the work involved and thus give a realistic bid.

A comparison of before and after drawings readily shows how the basic structure of the barn governed most of the new work. By using such studies the architect was able to take full advantage of the views. During the summer one can look out from any room to the woods and fields without setting eyes on another dwelling.

7

5

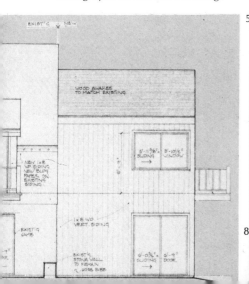

8

Many people who undertake barn remodelings plan to do a great deal of the work themselves, except for what must be done by licensed professionals. For some it has become a husband and wife or family weekend project for years, as the following pages illustrate.

Obviously, a lot of money can be saved in this way. Another benefit is that although progress may be slow, there is a deep sense of personal accomplishment when the job is finished.

The discovery of an abandoned barn or a farm for sale is the beginning of nearly every barn-owner's adventure in remodeling. The trials and tribulations from that point on are almost always similar. With minor variations, most barn conversions resemble the following account of the author's own experience.

My wife, Karen, her uncle, and I were out looking for a barn in the Hunter Mountain area of New York. We had just seen one that had been recommended to us by a friend; it sat within five feet of the road and within one foot of a property line, and would have had to be moved. Discouraged, we headed home. On the way, we happened past a site with a stone fireplace marking the remains of a burned-out house (1). Also visible from the road was the cupola of a barn (2).

We investigated further. Finding the property deserted and not posted, we discovered a magnificent old T-shaped barn (3). We tried to enter by way of the main sliding door, but to no avail (5). The large door had not been used in many years and did not budge.

So we explored the perimeter of the barn and found easy access on the lower level (4). Inside, we found ceiling beams cut from giant trees and walls made of native stone. We climbed steep wooden stairs (7) which led to the main hay storage area and found dramatic interior space (8, 9). Parts of the roof were missing and rays of light were filtering into the dim interior.

It was love at first sight. Before the day was over, we had opened our picnic basket and were sitting in the barnyard (our future patio) discussing how we would remodel the barn (6). Only then did it occur to us that it might not be for sale. We asked neighbors about the owner of the property and were discouraged to find that no one really knew much about it.

After searching for many weeks, we found a real estate firm that had once had a listing on the old farm. They contacted the owner and arranged the purchase of the property.

4

7

8

9
61

10

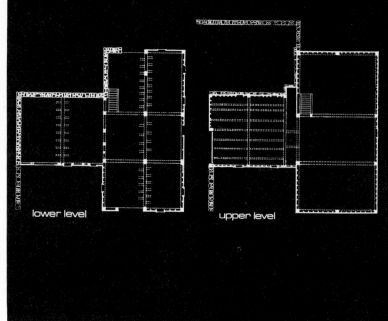

lower level upper level

14

11

12

Plans began by taking pictures of the barn from a distance to get the true relationships of the height and placement of the openings (10). When such photos, taken at right angles to each exterior face of the building, are enlarged to a known dimension, they clearly show the existing conditions.

We also took accurate measurements of the exterior with a tape and then enlarged our pictures in proportion to these overall dimensions. Inside, starting in one corner and taking successive measurements of the main columns and window openings, we arrived at a series of dimensions that we drew up to represent the plan of the existing barn (14). To verify the dimensions of the height, we used the same technique with a ladder to get to the top of the building. While on the ladder, we gained considerable information about the interior by taking pictures in every direction, including up toward the cupola (13). Again, the pictures must be taken at right angles to the walls (11) and not obliquely (12). When enlarged, they can help establish relationships more accurately than some measurements. In a picture of an end wall (15), for example, one can trace off the main beams, the diagonal bracing, and each 2-by-4 stud, if necessary, all to exact size and placement. Of course, one can do all the measurement by hand without the use of the camera, but the combination of the two methods will insure accuracy. From these photos and measurements we drew up the existing conditions of the exterior and interior and used them as the basis for design sketches and construction drawings (16, 17).

13

15

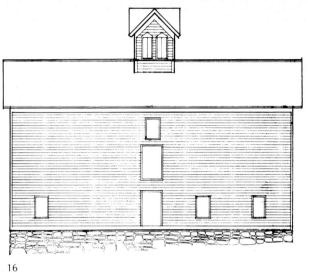

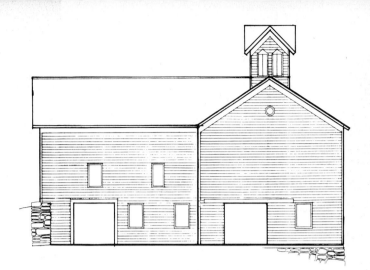

16

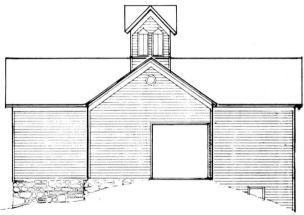

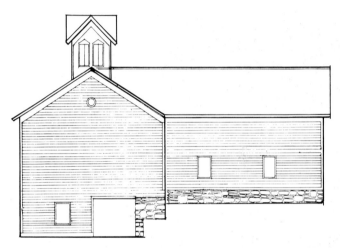

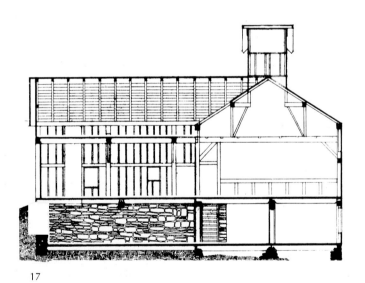

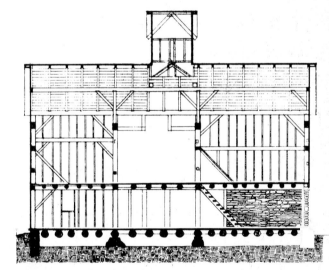

17

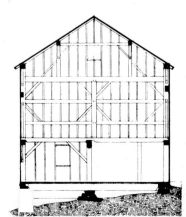

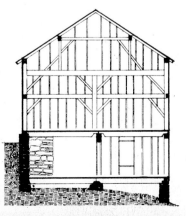

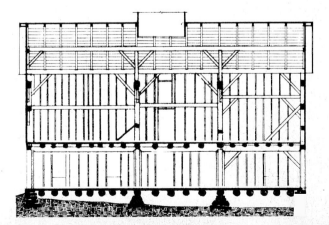

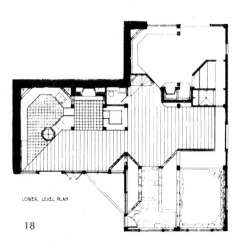

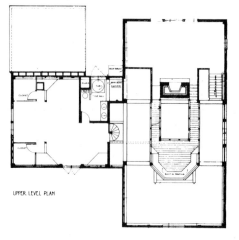

LOWER LEVEL PLAN   MIDDLE LEVEL PLAN   UPPER LEVEL PLAN

18

In the construction drawings, which should be made by an architect, it is advisable to have all levels of the plans and elevations drawn to the same scale (18, 19). These drawings can be used to secure financing and accurate bids from contractors on the total job. However, many conditions cannot always be predicted in any renovation, especially in structures as old as most barns. Walls may not be plumb, even though they appear to be. Hand-hewn beams and columns are not al-

ways easy to work with, and will necessitate a lot of extra cutting and fitting of new material to join the old. Therefore, in many cases the drawings must clearly show the intent of the construction (20), taking into account that many problems will have to be worked out on the job as they develop. If you are doing the work yourself with the help of a local carpenter, be prepared for almost endless unforeseen conditions. Sometimes drawings are not as useful as on-the-job decisions, and certainly a

combination of the two methods will occur in any case.

Because most barns were used for the storage of hay, windows are not usually abundant. In a renovation, however, windows are very important as they are needed to light up the vast interior spaces. Providing for them entails making the most drastic modification in the external appearance of the building. Replacing the vents in cupolas by windows provides an excellent way to get light streaming in through the roof.

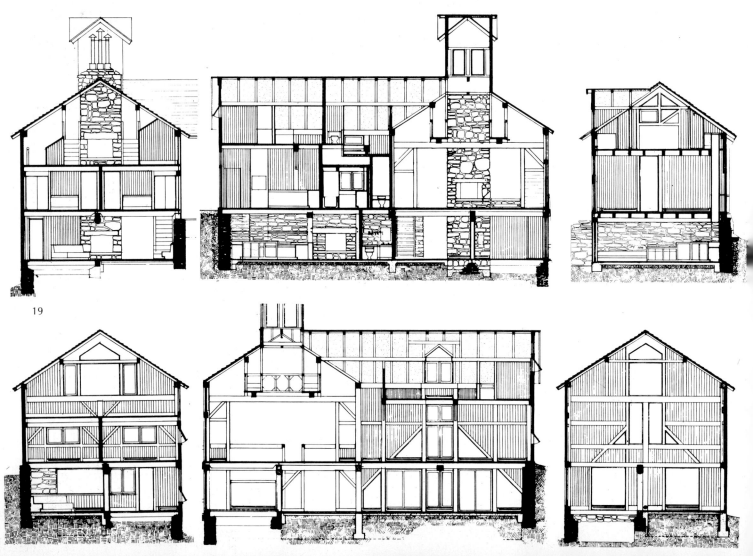

19

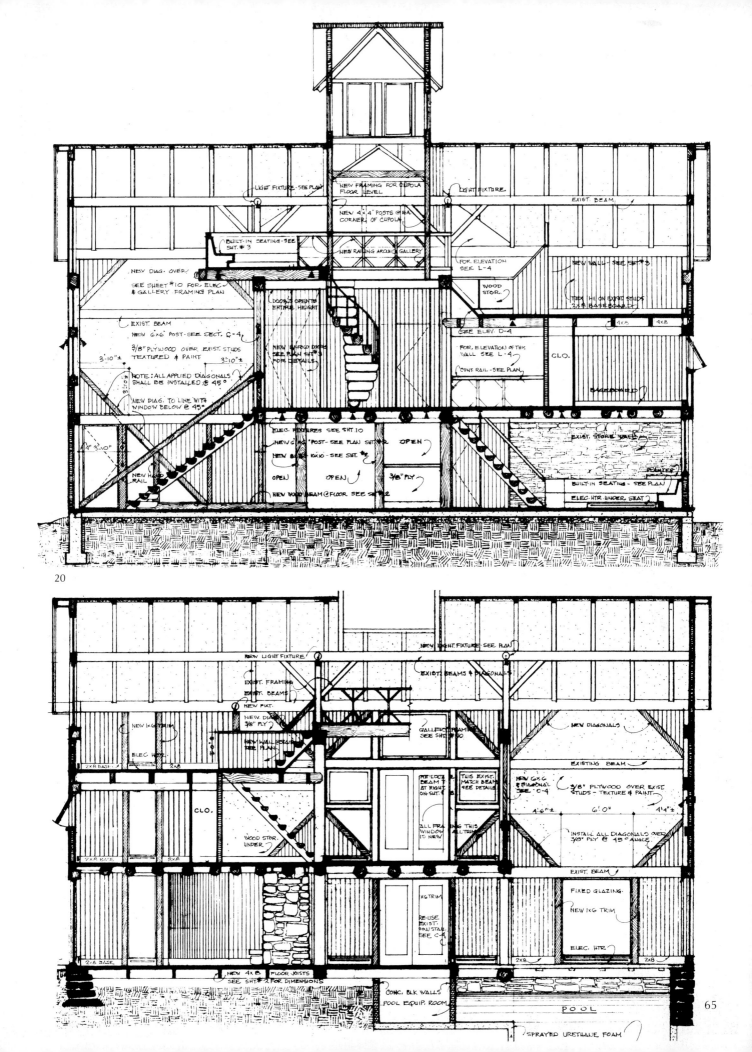

Upper section (drawing 20):

LIGHT FIXTURE - SEE PLAN
NEW FRAMING FOR CUPOLA FLOOR LEVEL
LIGHT FIXTURE
NEW 4"x4" POSTS @ EA. CORNER OF CUPOLA
EXIST. BEAM
BUILT-IN SEATING - SEE SHT. #3
NEW RAILING AROUND GALLERY
FOR ELEVATION SEE L-4
NEW WALL - SEE SHT. #3
NEW DIAG. OVER.
WOOD STOR.
SEE SHEET #10 FOR ELEC. & GALLERY FRAMING PLAN
TEX. HT. ON EXIST. STUDS 2x8 BASEBOARD
DOORS OPEN TO ENTIRE HEIGHT
EXIST. BEAM
NEW 6"x6" POST - SEE SECT. C-4
3/8" PLYWOOD OVER EXIST. STUDS TEXTURED & PAINT
3'-10"±
3'-10"±
NEW WOOD DOORS SEE PLAN SHT. #3 FOR DETAILS
SEE ELEV. D-4
FOR ELEVATION OF THIS WALL SEE L-4
CONT. RAIL - SEE PLAN
CLO.
NOTE: ALL APPLIED DIAGONALS SHALL BE INSTALLED @ 45°
NEW DIAG. TO LINE WITH WINDOW BELOW @ 45
4'x3'-10"
ELEC. FIXTURES SEE SHT. 10
NEW 6"x6" POST - SEE PLAN SHT. #2
NEW BM. 10x10 - SEE SHT. #2
OPEN
NEW HAND RAIL
OPEN
OPEN
3/8" PLY
NEW WOOD BEAM @ FLOOR SEE SHT. #2
EXIST. STONE WALL
PLANTER
BUILT-IN SEATING - SEE PLAN
ELEC. HTR. UNDER SEAT

20

Lower section (drawing 65):

NEW LIGHT FIXTURE - SEE PLAN
NEW LIGHT FIXTURE
EXIST. BEAMS & DIAGONALS
EXIST. FRAMING
EXIST. BEAMS
NEW FIXT.
NEW DIAG. 3/8" PLY
NEW DIAGONALS
NEW 1x6 TRIM
GALLERY FRAMING SEE SHT. #10
ELEC. HTR.
NEW WALL - SEE PLAN
EXISTING BEAM
2x8 BASE
2x8
NEW 6x6 & DIAGONAL SEE C-4
3/8" PLYWOOD OVER EXIST. STUDS - TEXTURE & PAINT
RE-LOCATE BEAM TO RIGHT ON SHT.
THIS EXIST. MATCH BEAM SEE DETAILS
4'-6"±
6'-0"
4'-4"±
CLO.
INSTALL ALL DIAGONALS OVER 3/8" PLY @ 45° ANGLE
WOOD STOR. UNDER
ALL FRAMING THIS WINDOW IS NEW
2x8 BASE
2x8
1x6 TRIM
RE-USE EXIST. INSTALL SEE C-4
EXIST. BEAM
FIXED GLAZING.
NEW 1x6 TRIM
ELEC. HTR.
2x8 BASE
NEW 4x8 FLOOR JOISTS SEE SHT. #2 FOR DIMENSIONS
2x8
2x8
CONC. BLK. WALLS POOL EQUIP. ROOM
POOL
SPRAYED URETHANE FOAM

65

The transformation of our barn into a residence can be seen by comparing a watercolor painting by Brian Burr (21) with a pencil rendering by the author (pp. 58–59) and with a view of the construction (24–26).

A rough study model (22) was made by using the new exterior elevations (23). These were pasted onto ¼-inch foam board, then cut out and assembled. It was helpful in studying the relationships of the exterior window patterns. The most pleasing view of the model was enlarged and used as the basis for the pencil perspective sketch. The exterior elevations were modified not by external conditions, but by designing the openings around the interior structure.

23

24

25

26

67

27

28

29

30

31

32

33

One of the inevitable steps in reconstruction is locating replacement timbers, either to repair damaged areas or to blend new work with that existing (27). If the project is in barn country, it is little trouble to scout the countryside in search of timbers (28). We were fortunate to find two sources. In one, two long 12-by-12 hand-hewn beams taken from a barn several years ago were stored. The second was a barn, belonging to a relative in another state, that had recently collapsed into a giant pile (29). Many of the pieces had to be cut to be removed (30). After a day's work, the result was a trailerload of small timbers for re-use.

In our barn the roof was the first part to be repaired. The existing roof was in very bad condition and had to be removed. After stripping the existing shingles, we covered the entire area with plywood, which stiffened and strengthened the structure. Over that, a new cedar shake roof was installed.

Much of the foundation of our barn was below grade. The stonework that formed the lower level was laid up without mortar (31) and in places the foundation wall was more than 2 feet thick. Since the lower level was to be our future kitchen and dining area, it was necessary to insulate and waterproof this entire wall.

First, a ditch was dug with a backhoe to a level below the lowest floor. Drain tile was installed at the bottom of the ditch and all large holes in the wall were plugged up with smaller rocks. The entire outer surface was then professionally sprayed with urethane foam which filled in and sealed all the openings (32). The foam was coated with tar for additional waterproofing and the ditch was filled back in. Thus the stonework was preserved on the interior and the wall was insulated and waterproofed at the same time.

The lower floor had housed cattle and horses and had to be thoroughly cleaned out; layers of debris and dirt were removed. At this point all the lower timbers were exposed as repair work was done to all the foundation sill plates (33). After this was completed, several loads of gravel were brought in and the earth prepared for a new complete floor. Foundations were poured for a fireplace and one new section of foundation was installed below grade using concrete block. After several beams and columns had been replaced and part of the structure jacked back into place, the major structural repairs were complete.

The entire interior of the barn was then prepared to receive urethane foam insulation. Beams were wrapped with plastic and masking tape; then ceiling, walls, and the inside of all stone foundations were sprayed with the foam. Its sealing qualities make it one of the best possible insulation materials. When a section of the roof was cut out for the fireplace later on, we could see how the foam had penetrated each space in the ceiling (37).

The existing hay lift track came in handy more than once during the construction, in lifting and moving scaffolding back and forth for working on the ceiling and later in setting the prefab metal fireplace on the upper level (38). The track and trolley are now a part of the completed job.

The most important modification to the inside appearance came when the dark, enclosed interior was opened for the installation of windows and glass areas. Each opening had been planned to coincide with the main structural members, so it was a simple matter to cut the openings (34–36). Since many of the glass openings were triangular and not a standard size, I decided to try ¼-inch acrylic sheets as an experimental form of glazing. The light weight of the material meant that all the irregular pieces could be cut on the spot and installed easily. Acrylic sheets have a much higher insulation factor than standard single glazing and the saving over glass is enormous. An additional consideration is their resistance to breakage either by wind or by vandals, a very important factor for a second home.

For many months we had worked in a dark, completely enclosed barn. Peeling the backing off the windows (39, 40) to let light stream inside and to suddenly see outdoors was a memorable turning point in the renovation of our barn.

34

35

36

38

37

39

40

Many barn-owners live in their new home as they work on it, once plumbing and some heat are installed. The inconvenience of living with construction going on is usually outweighed by being able to work at your own pace and by seeing accomplishments as they occur.

Dominique Storm van Leeuwen, owner of a prefabrication company, Barn Homes, and his family live in a barn in Woodstock, N.Y., which they have been working on for several years. It was originally close to the road, but Storm van Leeuwen moved it intact (p. 42). Once located on its permanent foundation, the plumbing was installed and restoration of the interior spaces was begun.

One of the first areas to be completed was the kitchen (1). Glass doors were installed to make use of its southern exposure. To utilize from the start the barn's three levels, Storm

van Leeuwen built a stairway and has finished it one side at a time (2, 3). To finish the surfaces he nailed an asbestos-type board throughout the interior to the existing frame, including the ceiling. Over this he applied a rough-textured stucco, leaving all the heavy timbers exposed.

On the high upper levels are the bedrooms, one of them reached by ladder like a hayloft, and from these one can look down on the living area (4, 5).

For Storm van Leeuwen, the freedom to adapt and adjust the building to suit his needs as he goes along outweighs the disadvantages of living in an unfinished barn.

2

4

5

3

When architect James Byron Bell decided to buy a barn for a second home in Accord, N.Y., he was looking for a large building within which he could build spaces for himself and his wife to live. The exterior remains exactly as he found it, with the exception of a wooden bridge built to provide access from the upper levels to a meadow (1, 2).

The interior is another story. Here he has built hanging platforms and walkways, some reachable only by ladder, and attached them all to the interior barn frame. Left unfinished, the frame serves essentially as a shell for these living spaces.

On the lowest level at grade, Bell

3

enclosed a small kitchen area (4) which is the only heated space in the building. The ceiling is made of removable Styrofoam panels to open up the space in warmer weather. The entire vertical space of the barn can then be seen from below or above (6).

Inside the main interior he has hung ropes, sculptures, and banners to create a movable environment (3). The interior spaces will thus always be changing as the Bells acquire new artifacts or found objects. Since none of the areas is truly enclosed, the space becomes articulated by these balconies and platforms. On one platform is pitched a tent which serves as the Bells' bedroom (5).

74

CHAPTER 7
Commercial Adaptations

Many potentially valuable barns that are in the path of suburban development may not be suitable for residences due to their large size or to encroaching commercial zoning. It is also usually impractical to move them. But we can no longer afford to tear down irreplaceable structures such as the ones shown in this chapter. The obvious answer, then, is to make them useful again through renovation and adaptive commercial re-use.

1

2

3

Ohio C. Barber, often referred to as the "match king," founded the city of Barberton, Ohio, in 1891. Here between 1904 and 1915 he built his 3,500-acre estate, the Anna Dean Farm, which he wished to make a model of scientific farming.

When completed, the farm consisted of 30 "French colonial" style buildings, constructed of red brick, white concrete block, and red tile roofs. The first and smallest of the barns is 300 feet long (1, 2, 4). Its most distinguishing feature is the tower silo (3), copied from a feudal castle in Luxemburg.

Unfortunately, Barber spent so much money in the building of this fabulous estate that the farm never paid for itself. When he died, it was divided up and sold.

Today, only 8 of the original buildings remain. Even the elaborate 40-room mansion is gone, having been razed in 1965. The first barn constructed is the last one remaining, and many efforts have been made to save it from the fate of the others.

The Barberton Historical Society managed to get the barn listed on the National Register of Historic Places in 1973. However, numerous development schemes for the property have been proposed, and although most of them have fallen through, the fate of the barn is still in question.

Barns of this historic significance must be preserved, if not as museums or showplaces, then at least as adaptations for other uses.

4

Hancock Shaker Village, near Pittsfield, Mass., has been a public museum since 1968.

Its most famous building, the round stone barn (1), was built in 1826 to house 52 head of cattle, and to store hay. It is a pioneering and often imitated example of what we today call functionalism.

The top level allowed access for the hay wagons which traversed the interior on a balcony, where the hay was dumped down a central chute. The middle level held the milking stanchions, which radiated around the central manger so that the cattle could be fed by a single hand. Manure was shoveled through trapdoors to the open-air bottom level.

Cooperstown, N.Y., is a town of museums, housing the Baseball Hall of Fame, the James Fenimore Cooper Home, and several others. Here a castlelike barn (2) has been successfully converted into the Farmers' Museum, a showplace of early American tools and other objects of farm life. Another such display can be found at the Eric Sloane Museum in Cornwall, Conn., which was built to resemble a barn.

ENTRANCE

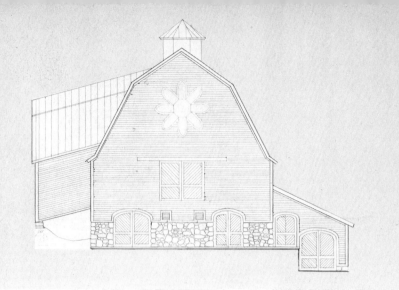

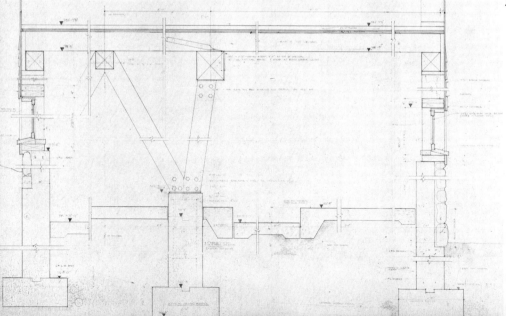

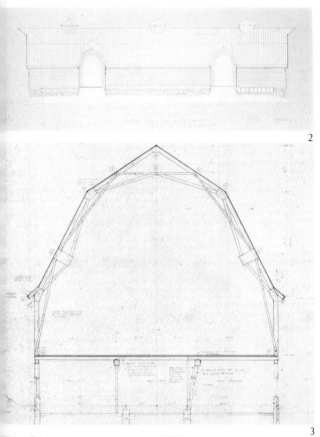

It is not often that an architect receives a commission to design a cow barn. But architect Moritz Bergmeyer is doing just that in Enosburg Falls, Vt., and he considers it one of his most challenging opportunities (1, 2).

The owner wanted a barn that could withstand the harsh winter climate of extreme northern Vermont (9). Most barns in the area ultimately collapse because they were not built so that the wind forces are distributed through the structure to the lower-level foundations.

A second determining factor in the design was the limited availability of lumber in the area. Restricted to 16-foot-long pieces, Bergmeyer designed an elaborate truss system that carries out the classic form of the Dutch gambrel roof (5, 7, 11). The span of the trusses is 48 feet and the overall length of the barn is 200 feet. The stress of the upper trusses is carried down to the foundations in the 8-by-8 bracing on the lower level (4, 6). The architect simply took a traditional barn shape and continued the en-

gineering analysis to insure continued stability.

To enable the owner to drive a tractor and hay wagon right into the barn, Bergmeyer designed two entryways, called "wharfing," which became separate design elements that also related to the Dutch gambrel roof design (2, 3).

The owner, an art student as well as a dairy farmer, has incorporated many specially designed works of art into the design of the barn and the farm in general. At the entrance gate, one is greeted with an attractive painted sign. The lower level of the barn, containing the stalls, has a ceramic tile mosaic of a cow form. At one end of the main or storage level is a round stained-glass window of a colorful pastoral scene (8). The cupola will be topped by a weather vane 8 feet in diameter, which is being designed by a sculptor.

To celebrate the completion of construction, the owner held a traditional barn dance, which was attended by nearly 5,000 people (10).

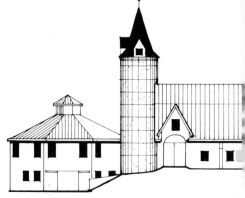

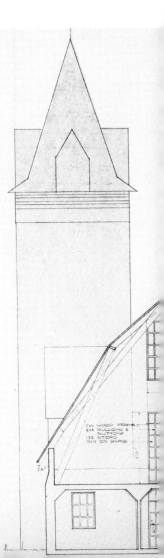

The Ganahl Dairy Barn in Ballwin, Mo., was one of the largest modern dairies in the United States. Built of stone and brick in the early 1920s, it resembles a medieval castle and was once the show place of a 1,000-acre farm (1, 2). After a fire extensively damaged the abandoned barn in 1968, it was scheduled for razing.

Many promoters had plans for the site, but none materialized until developer Paul Londe proposed to restore the landmark as the nucleus of a

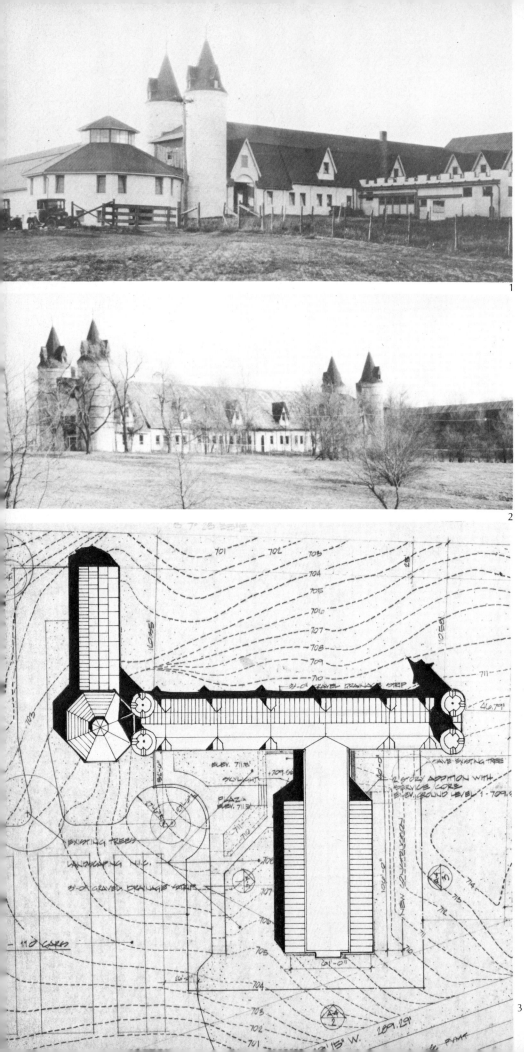

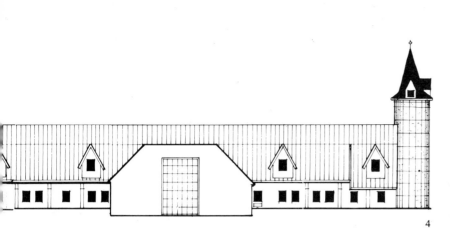

4

large shopping center. His plans called for totally preserving its architectural character and design (4, 5). In the first phase he intended to restore the barn to include a restaurant, specialty shops, and art galleries. The barn was then to be surrounded by a large shopping mall (3).

Once the necessary permits were obtained and Londe's plans approved, the building sat unused for two years, during which time vandals reduced the grand landmark nearly to

rubble. However, once the restoration began (6, 7), public interest in the project picked up and several spaces were leased. The octagonal room at one end of the barn (8) has been converted into a restaurant and bar. One silo will be used for a private dining area.

With the heritage and history of the barn to build upon, and with many renovation problems now solved, the new facility will bring a new life to the community.

6

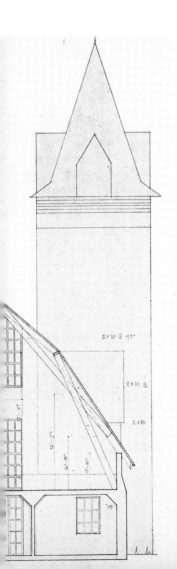

5

7

8

1

The present owner of this rejuvenated barn in Fredericksburg, Va., moved here in 1957. The large barn (1) became the focal point of many family and community activities. Since then it has been converted into the restaurant, lounge, and banquet hall of a Sheraton Motor Inn (3). The conversion demanded considerable rebuilding and presented many problems, but both architects Edward Sinnott & Son and the owner believe that the result justified the expense.

There have been several additions to the original barn, including an extension of the restaurant (2). The bar is located next to one of the silos,

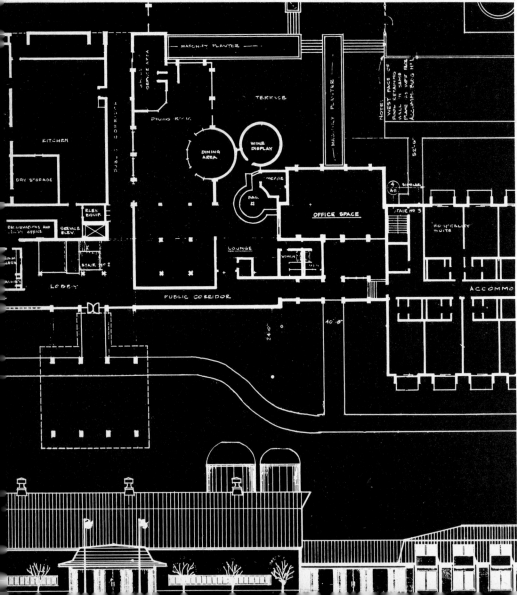

3

which was made into a private dining room. The large upper hayloft area serves as banquet facilities. Although all the original siding was replaced, the roof remains intact.

The new portion of the structure, consisting of motel units, was added in a long low building that wraps around the central swimming pool (4, 6). This building is visible from the restaurant. Its roof forms were designed to reflect the angle and texture of the original barn (5), for a very harmonious effect. Shortly after completion the renovation was designated "top property" in the Sheraton chain.

1

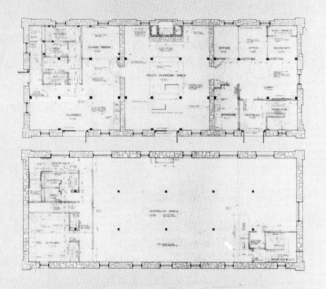

2

This Maryland stone carriage house was built in 1830 for a gentleman farmer. It was recently purchased by the Kittamaqundi Community in Columbia, a nondenominational Christian community, as its center. The new owner's intent is to make minimum modifications and to adapt the existing spaces and character to the new use (1, 2). Architect Neil Lang has tried to limit design changes to those that can be handled one by one as funds become available.

The stone walls, approximately 18 inches thick, are left exposed on both sides. All the old stall doors were refitted and remain as original. New doors were designed to match the existing ones. All exterior openings were maintained in their original locations and refitted with standard

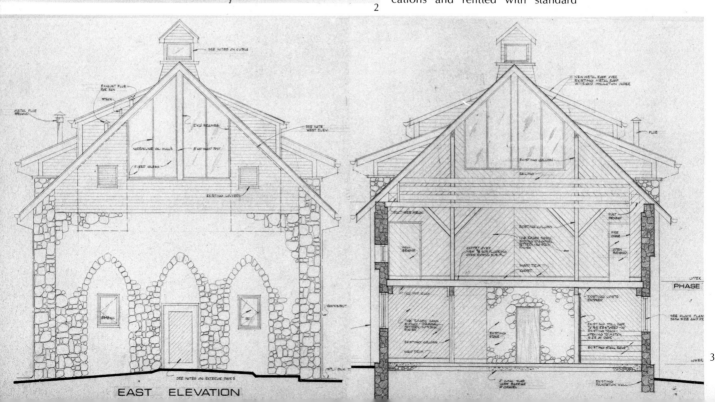

EAST ELEVATION

PHASE

3

windows (3, 4). To date, first-floor renovation of the Kittamaqundi project is nearly complete while the upper floors are awaiting funding, which comes from private sources.

Many decisions have been made in the field through a good working relationship among the owner, contractor, and the architect.

4

1

A dog kennel on a large estate near Plainfield, Conn., now functions as a community recreation center. It was redesigned in conjunction with a multifamily housing development by architect Lee Harris Pomeroy (1).

The upper level, which now contains a large recreation area, was once a hayloft. The dog pens were located on the middle level, now the lobby, and the lower level was used for storage. The wooden trusses of the original heavy timber construction remain exposed in the new design. The exterior, originally clad in cedar shingles, has been restored with vertical wood siding (2). The tower is used for observation, but is not open to the public.

2

85

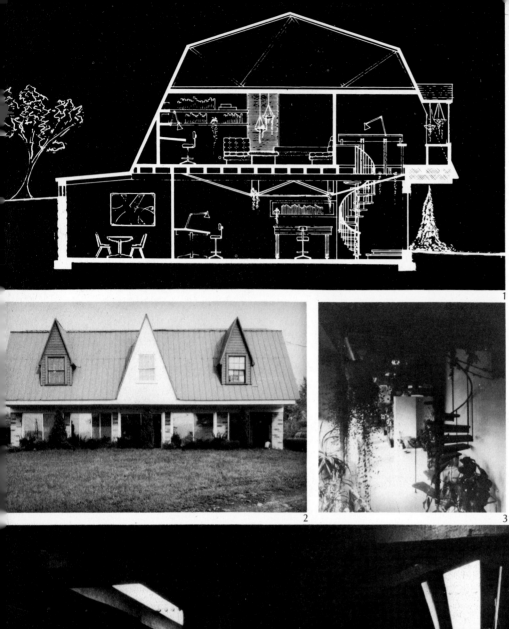

Commercial restoration has also been done on a private level. Recycling and adaptive use are fast becoming guidelines for many architects.

Architects Liebman and Hurwitz have restored a barn for use as their own office near New Paltz, N.Y. The column-free space is achieved by the ingenious truss system of the original barn (1, 4). A new stairway (3) leads to the living space and additional offices above. The changes made to the exterior were minor and did not affect the overall appearance (2).

Another recycling project by the same firm utilized the shell of an old barn in Liberty, N.Y., to house new offices for an audiovisual production company (5, 7). The original trusswork was left exposed throughout, thus creating a two-story lobby level with a flow of space (6, 8, 9).

4

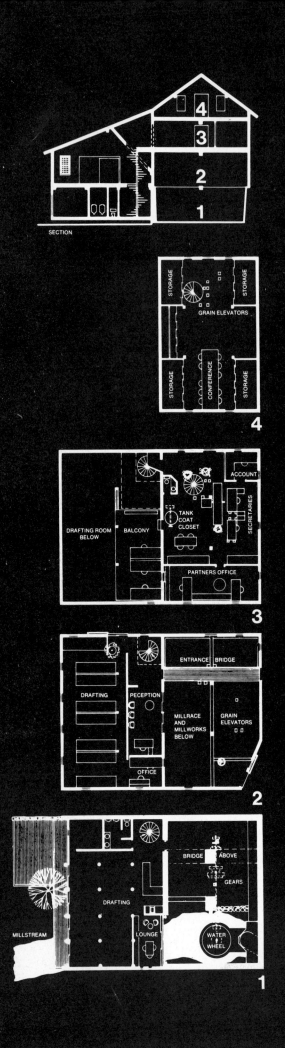

SECTION

4

STORAGE · STORAGE

GRAIN ELEVATORS

STORAGE · CONFERENCE · STORAGE

4

ACCOUNT

SECRETARIES

DRAFTING ROOM BELOW · BALCONY

TANK COAT CLOSET

PARTNERS OFFICE

3

ENTRANCE BRIDGE

DRAFTING · PECEPTION

MILLRACE AND MILLWORKS BELOW · GRAIN ELEVATORS

OFFICE

2

BRIDGE ABOVE

GEARS

DRAFTING

MILLSTREAM

LOUNGE · WATER WHEEL

1

On a morning when he could no longer face another 90-minute commute to New York City, landscape architect Robert Zion determined to relocate his office and bought a condemned mill for sale in his own town of Imlaystown, N.J. Thus began a major project for the mill and for Zion.

Built in 1695, the mill was owned by Richard Salter, an ancestor of Lincoln. In 1898 fire destroyed portions of it, but it was rebuilt and continued to operate until 1962. The restoration (1, 2) is actually a double recycling project because Zion and his partner Harold Breen not only saved the building by turning it into office space, but provided for its eventual return to milling. The equipment visible in the photographs is not mere decoration. The offices have been designed to nestle in and surround the existing elements of the mill (5–9).

The entrance is particularly dramatic (6). From the street a door opens on to a bridge, which Zion & Breen built across the open millrace. Crossing the bridge, one can look down on the old horizontal water wheel and the 1695 stone foundation walls and listen to the mill stream, which still flows through the structure. On the far side is the entrance to the office space which is distributed on four levels.

At entrance level are the reception area (3) and main drafting room (4). On the second floor are the partners' offices. A spiral stair cut into a former grain bin provides access to this area and to the third floor, which contains a conference room. The lower level contains an employees' lounge.

Where possible, the original structure of the building is revealed and highlighted by bold colors. Simple furniture and occasional partitions and cabinets in bright colors provide a modern, clear counterpart to the antique charm.

All of the floors are distinguished by the old mill machinery, which would be fascinating as pure sculpture but takes on special significance because it symbolizes both the structure's past and its possible future as a grist mill. The original machinery has been cleaned and reconditioned. The few pieces that have been removed or changed could be easily replaced.

2

5

6

3

8

7

9

89

1

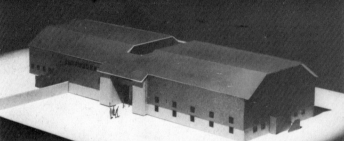

2

3

4

The Darrow School is on the site of the original Shaker Church Family in the Shaker Village in Lebanon, N.Y. (1, 4). It has been in use since 1932.

Architect James Baker attended the Darrow School from 1944 to 1950 and is now a member of the board of trustees. In 1963 he and George Lewis renovated an old Shaker dairy barn into an auditorium and theater for the school (2, 3).

Since then Baker has designed a completely new science building adjacent to the barn (5, 6). It contains classrooms, laboratories, and a greenhouse. Its exterior, as with all buildings in the Shaker Village, is plain and unadorned. The bold simplicity and relationship of building masses make its roots immediately recognizable.

5

6

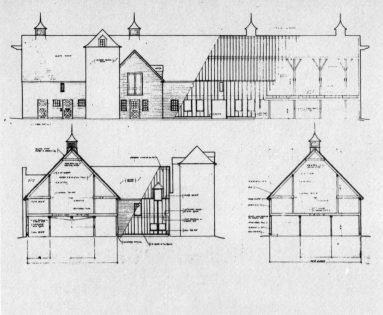

This barn was built in 1930 by the former owner of Montpelier Manor, Md. (1). The manor itself is pre-revolutionary. The barn, once used as a stable and for grain storage, will soon find new life as a visual arts center and workshop for the Maryland National Capitol Parks and Planning Commission.

Preliminary design work by architect Neil Lang shows the extent of alterations to the existing structure (2–4). Tests were carried out to determine if the desired structural changes were feasible and if the barn could reasonably be converted to a 200- to 300-person assembly area, including support systems.

This recycled small dairy barn in Greenwich, Conn., houses a gallery and studios for drawing, painting, ceramics, and jewelry-making (1, 3). Rather than developing finished spaces, architect Tom Kupper simply let the structure of the barn serve as the main architectural element (2). It is slowly being transformed as usable studio space is required.

With an elaborate budget, the entire project could have been finished in months, but then some of the charm of the Art Barn would have been lost. The lower level, which housed the cattle, is being successfully used as the main gallery. There is no doubt that the visitor is in a remade cow barn, but perhaps that is what makes the gallery space so interesting.

These buildings, known as the Lansing Manor complex (2, 3), were acquired by the New York State Power Authority for transformation into an educational and scientific center (1). It adjoins the Mine Kill State Park, created by the Power Authority as part of the Blenheim-Gilboa Pumped Storage Power Project. Restoration (4, 5) was undertaken by the Power Authority with the cooperation of the Schoharie County Historical Society.

The most famous building, projected as a museum, is the Victorian-era Lansing Manor House, which is listed in the National Register of Historic Places. The visitors' center (6) occupies a restored barn. The silo has been adapted for use as a weather station and for scientific displays.

4

In the basement of the barn a theater offers periodic multimedia presentations. An observatory built on the rear of the barn enables visitors to view the sweeping panorama of the valley and the reservoir. Exhibits were designed so as to retain and enhance the openness and character of the original barn interior.

5

transmission

the final
path of
electricity

6

95

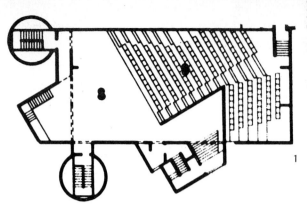

1

The Simon's Rock Art Center in Great Barrington, Mass., consists of two parts, a 200-seat theater and an art barn which houses painting and sculpture studios. Of the angled additions to the sides of the old dairy barn, it is the theater that contributes most (2–4). The drama school needed a stage with a long leading edge because most of the teaching involves movement, dance, and drama.

By setting the stage on the diagonal, architects Hardy Holzman Pfeiffer increased its potential length by ten feet (1). The seating naturally follows along the same bias, and the protrusions are extensions for access and additional light. Thus the plan has a certain consistent logic. In addition, a large skylight was extended up from the ridge of the main gambrel. The rear stage extension was also given generous amounts of glass in order to illuminate the performance area by day (5).

2

3

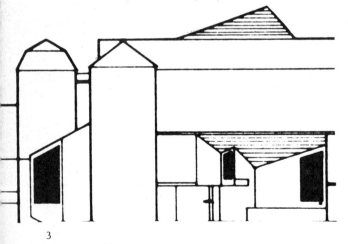

4

5

In the town of Lockport, N.Y., which grew up around the locks of the Erie Canal, this carriage house was built in 1850. It underwent three major renovations before being purchased for a community theater.

The exterior is of brick with slightly recessed windows; the slate roof is topped with a cupola. The original structure has largely been retained and repaired by Hardy Holzman Pfeiffer (1). A cantilevered stage was raised above the existing floor level (2). The seating, like the stage, is built up on wood-framed platforms. Above the seating hangs a round enameled air duct. Rods suspended from the open roof structure carry adjustable stage lighting (3, 4). The large cupola and all existing windows were repaired and reglazed.

1

3

2

4

Designer William Schickel has been involved with various barn projects for over 25 years. In 1958 he redesigned the Grailville Oratory in Loveland, Ohio. The original structure, probably 150 years old, was a magnificent large barn with unique clerestory windows that Schickel rebuilt.

On the interior, white sand-finish plaster walls accentuate the dark timbers (3). The altar, communion table, and lectern are set apart on a platform surrounded by the dark stained wood floor (2). The lectern is made of pine and black iron. The altar is made of pine and mahogany laminated strips.

Vertical board-and-batten, painted white, was applied to the exterior. On the new facade, a sheet metal hood shelters the main doors (1), which are reached by a raised ramp.

Inside the Chain O'Lakes Convenant Church in McHenry, Ill., the original beams and fieldstone walls are still there, sandblasted to their natural state. Outside, the modified silolike structure confirms that this church was once a barn (1). A restricted budget was the main reason for its conversion into a sanctuary and fellowship hall.

Architects Rowe, Abplanalp & Johnson cut the roof of the existing silo on an angle to blend with the new spire. At the top is the skylighted pastor's study, and below that the church office. The location and spacing of the original columns suggested the arrangement of the 200-seat sanctuary (3, 4). The communion table is set up on four old barn timbers (2), and around it on three sides are grouped the pews.

The entire building has a rustic, natural tone inside and out. The exterior is rough-sawn red cedar siding, which retains the feeling of the original barn red.

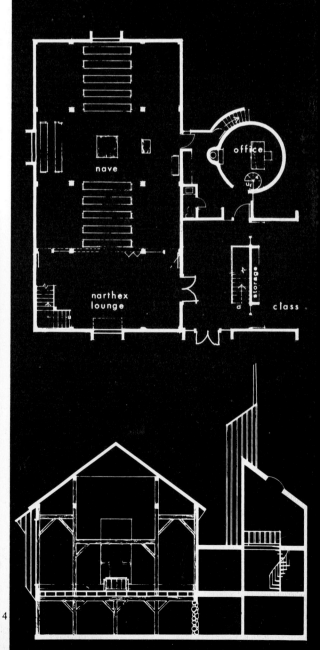

PART TWO
Barns for Living

CHAPTER 8
Barn Homes

A good many people undertake barn remodelings with the help of a builder. There are many ways to go about converting a barn into a functional, warm, and comfortable house. On the following pages, each owner has approached the problem differently, yet each one has found a sympathetic contractor or builder who has shared his or her enthusiasm. For a truly successful result this mutual understanding is essential.

1

2

3

Richard Babcock doesn't simply fix up old barns to make them habitable. Instead he acts more as an architect than a builder. He takes down barns, moves them to his customers' property, and puts them back together again on new concrete foundations. He himself lives in one of his own re-creations in the Berkshires.

He has completed 28 such reconstructions in the past 20 years, and he continues to seek out the 200-year-old Dutch barns, which are his favorites. All hand-hewn, these barns usually have massive beams, some measuring 18 by 24 inches. They are also the only barns in existence that have a mortise-and-tenon joint where

4

5

6

the tenon protrudes beyond the column and is pegged on the outside tongue (3).

Babcock asks a prospective barnhouse owner what features and how many rooms he wants. This lets him know how large a barn he will need to get. He usually has several different-size barns available, but often he will look for a specific barn to meet the needs of the future owner.

The new homes all have stone fireplaces which Babcock usually builds out of the original foundations. If that is impractical, he uses local stone.

The soaring ceiling of the original barn is always retained in the living rooms; and the kitchen, bathrooms, and bedrooms are designed in the opposite end of the structure.

Almost every barn needs a new roof to become habitable. The most authentic looking roof can be made from wood shingles. However, Babcock has gone one step further. In some cases, he salvages the original slate roof and carefully removes each piece. Then he puts a new plywood membrane over the beams and installs the old slate on the new building. Breakage of the old brittle slate is a problem, but a slate roof will outlast many other kinds.

1, 2. Clinton and Varney Elliot residence, Tyringham, Mass. 3. Lou and Patricia Benton residence, western Massachusetts. 4. Richard and Dorothy Lattizzori residence, Williamstown, Mass. 5. Richard Babcock residence, Hancock, Mass. .6. Milton and Francis Slater residence, Hancock, Mass. 7–9. Richard and Dorothy Stern residence, Hancock, Mass. 10. Edward and Muriel Wyner residence, Hancock, Mass.

105

1

One look at the interior of a Babcock barn reveals that he has painstakingly restored the entire frame to its original arrangement of columns and beams. His main concern is to have the symmetry of the original barn frame expressed in the new interior. This can be seen in two views of the Lattizzori residence (11, 12) and in the balcony view of the Wyner residence, overlooking the main living space (13).

2

3

1

2

Nestled in a green valley in the Catskill Mountains, this barn-house is the home of painter Natalia Hofmann (1). The barn was moved several miles piece by piece and reassembled adjoining a century-old stone house. The entryway is located between the two structures (2), and the main kitchen area (3) is directly off the entry on the ground level of the barn.

3

Hofmann's painting studio is inside the main barn space. Light from the large north windows filters throughout the entire room. The vast ceiling was sprayed with urethane foam insulation and then spray painted white. At one end stairs lead to a balcony loft (4), which is open and part of the main space. From here one can see the original wood-rung ladder that was used to reach the haymow (5).

Sparse and carefully selected furnishings give an almost Shaker simplicity to the studio, yet the natural light softens the wood colors.

When artist Susanne Mason walked into this previously converted Long Island barn, she felt that she had been there before — and indeed, she had seen pictures published several years before (1). It was originally renovated by Richard Heimann, who has since gone on to another barn renovation job.

What Mason brought to the project was a second barn taken from a farm in Pennsylvania where she grew up. She had the barn taken apart and shipped to the Long Island site, where it was connected with a doorway to one end of the existing building (2). This new space will serve as her painting studio (3). In the studio the ceiling has been plastered and painted white. She also had a large skylight installed to admit more light. In the main living space, the ceiling of the original barn is left exposed (4).

This stone-bank barn (1–3) in Riegelville, Pa., was transformed into a home and office by designer Donald Sarstedt with a little help from his architect friend William Callahan. The lower floor serves as his office. The main living area (4) is on the level that was once approached by a ramp. The original barn doors were re-used as shutters over the new windows, giving added insulation during winter. Thus Sarstedt retained the external character of the original barn while providing a convenient, warm interior for his family.

When interior designer Gina Beadle turned to real estate brokerage for her livelihood, she did not abandon her love of colorful and decorative surfaces. This is the most evident in her East Hampton home, a barn that had been moved from several miles away. On the south end are the kitchen and dining area (2). This part of the building is flooded with sunlight in the winter, yet cool and shaded in the summer.

Draperies, colorful wall decorations, and plants add to the warmth of the interior space, which is all on one main level without loft or balconies (1).

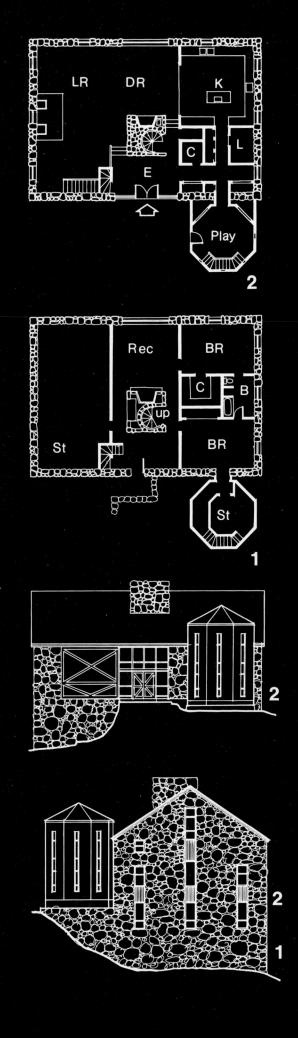

LR DR K

C L

E

Play

2

Rec BR

C B

up

St

St

1

2

2

1

2

3

This handsome stone barn near Copes Bridge, Pa., was once an ox-powered grist mill, and at one time a wind-powered mill (1, 2, 5). Although its age is uncertain, it is over a century old. The stone walls are more than 2 feet thick.

It took contractor William Rolland over seven months to do this rewarding renovation (3). The silo form, added to the mill around 1900, gives the exterior its distinctive shape (4). Rolland adapted the silo for his children's bedrooms on the upper level and a playroom below. The underground stone section of the silo contains a photographic darkroom and storage area.

Next to the entry and silo is the kitchen (7), which is located over the former grain room floor. All the cabinets are treated to leave the natural grain exposed and some counter tops are covered with hand-made ceramic tile. A portion of floor is also of handmade Mexican tile. The remaining floors are wood.

The most striking area is the living room where the stone walls and beams were sandblasted to their orig-

4

5

6

inal hues. In one corner (6) is a 12-foot-square block of masonry faced with limestone, which was taken from the exterior to make room for windows. Winding around this column is the main stairwell, patterned after barn stairs of the 1800 period. Three fireplaces and two log boxes are built into this masonry mass.

The main window area faces south so that the vast interior is filled with sunlight in the winter. The other windows were designed as narrow slots (8), in keeping with the traditional narrow ventilating openings of stone barns. The main entry door was patterned after sketches of early barn doors by Eric Sloane.

8

7

This barn in East Hampton, N.Y., is the second one that photographer Richard Heimann has redone with his wife, Sweater, and he is eagerly waiting for a chance to do another. Barns to him are the world's most exciting structural forms.

Realizing that the existing barn was too small for their needs, Heimann added on an upper-level bedroom area and a porch which he enclosed with glass skylights (1). Below are the kitchen and dining room, which are the main living portions of the house (2). This space can be closed off from the large living room, saving a great amount of heat. The main source of heat in the living room is provided by a stark modern fireplace with exposed plastered chimney flues (3).

Light streams in through the window wall, which faces the outdoor deck and a heavily wooded area. Heimann left the original ceiling boards in place and completely exposed. The furniture of soft leather and chrome provides a nice contrast to the rich warm colors of the barn timbers.

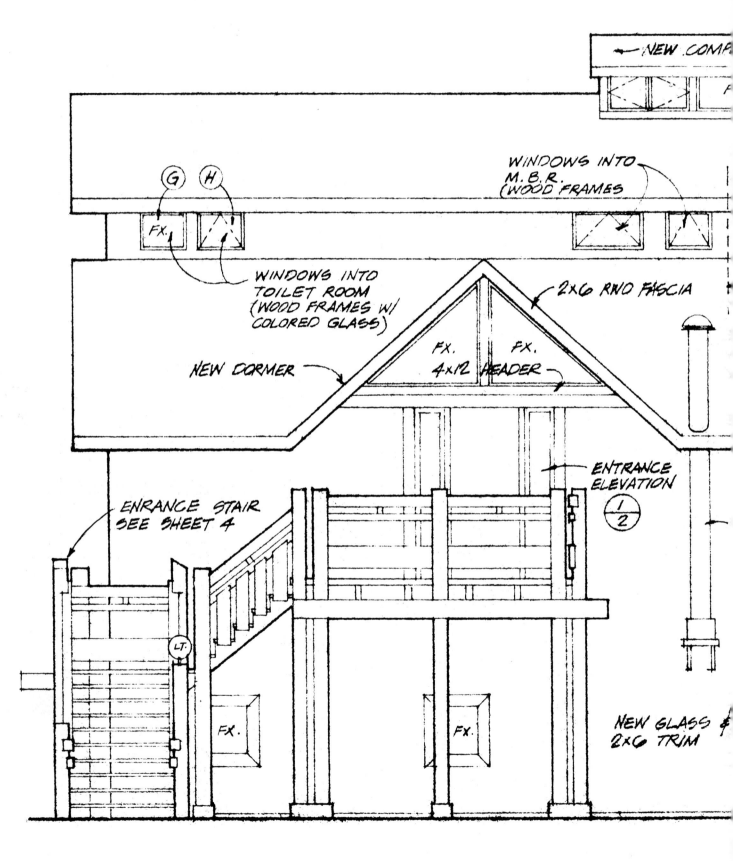

NEW COMP

WINDOWS INTO M.B.R. (WOOD FRAMES

Ⓖ Ⓗ

FX.

WINDOWS INTO TOILET ROOM (WOOD FRAMES W/ COLORED GLASS)

NEW DORMER

2x6 RWD FASCIA

FX.   FX.
4x12 HEADER

ENTRANCE ELEVATION

①
②

ENRANCE STAIR SEE SHEET 4

LT.

FX.

FX.

NEW GLASS & 2x6 TRIM

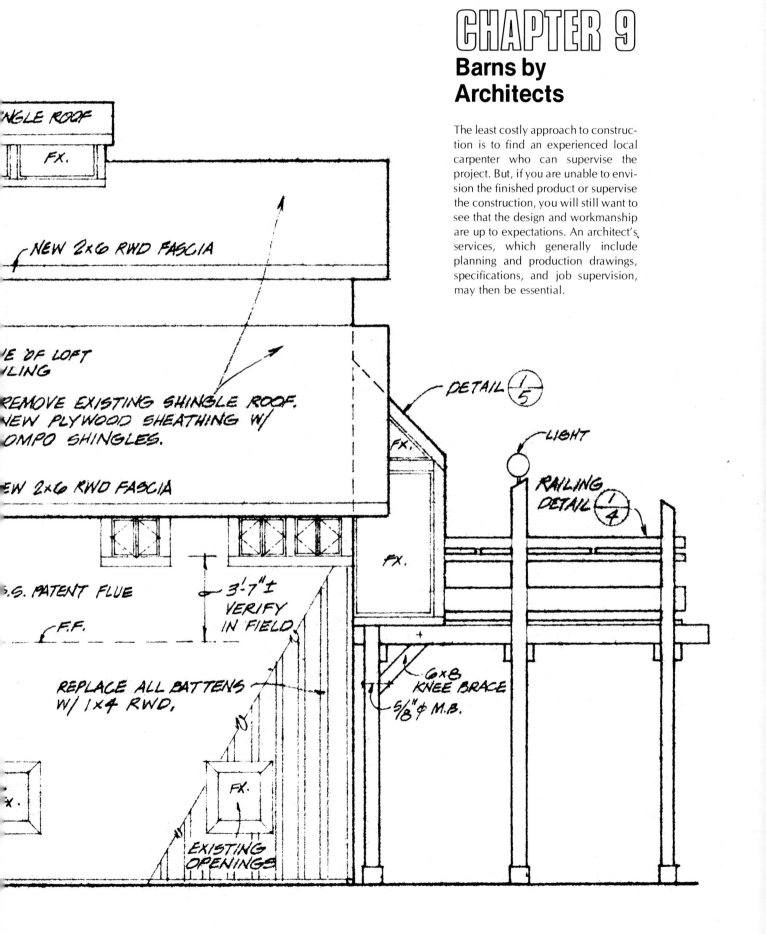

CHAPTER 9
Barns by Architects

The least costly approach to construction is to find an experienced local carpenter who can supervise the project. But, if you are unable to envision the finished product or supervise the construction, you will still want to see that the design and workmanship are up to expectations. An architect's services, which generally include planning and production drawings, specifications, and job supervision, may then be essential.

NGLE ROOF

FX.

NEW 2x6 RWD FASCIA

E OF LOFT
LING

REMOVE EXISTING SHINGLE ROOF.
NEW PLYWOOD SHEATHING W/
OMPO SHINGLES.

EW 2x6 RWD FASCIA

.S. PATENT FLUE

F.F.

REPLACE ALL BATTENS
W/ 1x4 RWD,

3'-7"±
VERIFY
IN FIELD

FX.

EXISTING
OPENINGS

DETAIL 1/5

LIGHT

RAILING
DETAIL 1/4

FX.

6x8
KNEE BRACE

5/8" ⌀ M.B.

Built of redwood over 50 years ago, this California wine country barn was acquired by a Bay Area couple as a weekend vacation home (3). They hired architect William Kirsch to help them in their ambitious project (1). His interest in recycling old buildings, old timbers, old stained-glass windows, and numerous other artifacts leads him to shift such items around from one building to another to extend their usefulness and beauty.

The barn was first stripped of its redwood siding, which was remilled to smooth the edges and then used for interior paneling and trim. New siding of construction-heart rough-sawn redwood board-and-batten replaced the old. (A full side elevation, with architect's notes, is shown on the preceding pages.)

Inside, Kirsch added a main-floor level (2) and above it a balcony loft for the master bedroom and bath. The ground floor is used for utilities and garage. On the outside he added two porches, which overlook the vineyard (4). This can be reached through a pair of Gothic arched doors, opening from the living room (5).

Kirsch believes that anyone who tackles a renovation has to determine how much he or she wishes to spend, and that the advantages of remodeling are both ecological and aesthetic. Re-using an old structure saves consuming new materials for an all new structure. He also adds that his clients enjoy living in a building that has had a previous life. Its age gives it a softness and mellowness that can never be found in a new house.

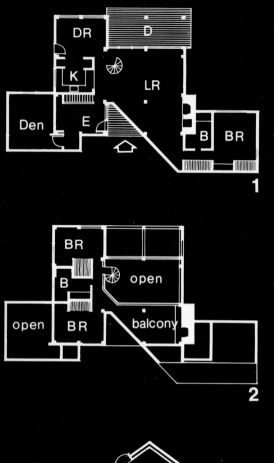

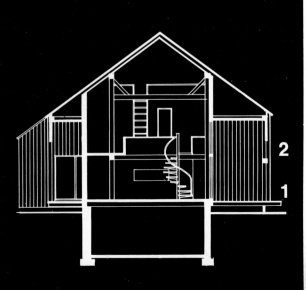

2

In designing this alteration in Ashfield, Mass., architects Juster Pope Associates broke within the rectangular barn frame to create a diagonal movement to the plan (1). The porch is recessed into the frame and this diagonal is also expressed in the roof line (2). Inside, a second-floor balcony adds to the sense of space (3).

In another barn-home conversion, in Conway, Mass., by the same firm (5), the barn was stripped down to the frame, moved, and put up on a new foundation. The design of the interior makes use of the cathedrallike space.

The shedlike forms added onto the exterior strongly reflect the vernacular of barn design (4).

3

4

5

There is no confusing the old and the new in this Charlotte, Vt., barn (1) that architect Tom Cullins remodeled into a year-round house for himself, his wife, Kelly, and their daughter, Sarah.

To begin with, the barn was a lovely shell with a beautiful relationship to the land, the town, and another farm building on the site. It was structurally sound and was well oriented to the sun, with one of its broad sides facing south.

The old is the original shell of oak, built around 1875 for hay storage. The new is mostly white and contemporary, definitely not rustic (2). The entire interior was sandblasted at the beginning of construction. This cleaned the old wood on the ceiling, which is left exposed, and brought out the warm toast color of the hand-hewn beams, and the vertical wall siding. Having such a huge space to heat, the architect decided to make use of solar heat by putting large glass doors (4) on the south as well as on the north. Ten feet square, they are located where the tractor and hay wagons used to enter. At night, to conserve heat and to provide additional privacy, they are closed off by new rolling doors. These doors, when opened in the summer, provide excellent cross ventilation.

Two people were important in the overall carrying out of the design. One was Kelly, who shared in many of the decisions. The other was Dennis Willmot, a student of architecture and a builder who understands what the renovation of a barn is all about. He was an immense help with the carrying out of the details.

In the furnishings the Cullinses included items that Vermont craftsmen could build, such as the butcher block counters and the wood stove. The furniture cluster in the living room is like a village square to them. The living room space is designed so that all the other rooms have views into this main social area (3, 5).

1. Main House
2. Workshop
3. Potting Shed
4. Pool House
5. Bath House
6. Pool
7. Future Sauna
8. Barn Hall
9. Storage
10. Wood Shed
11. Garage
12. Summer House
a. Living
b. Dining
c. Kitchen
d. Bedroom
e. Bath

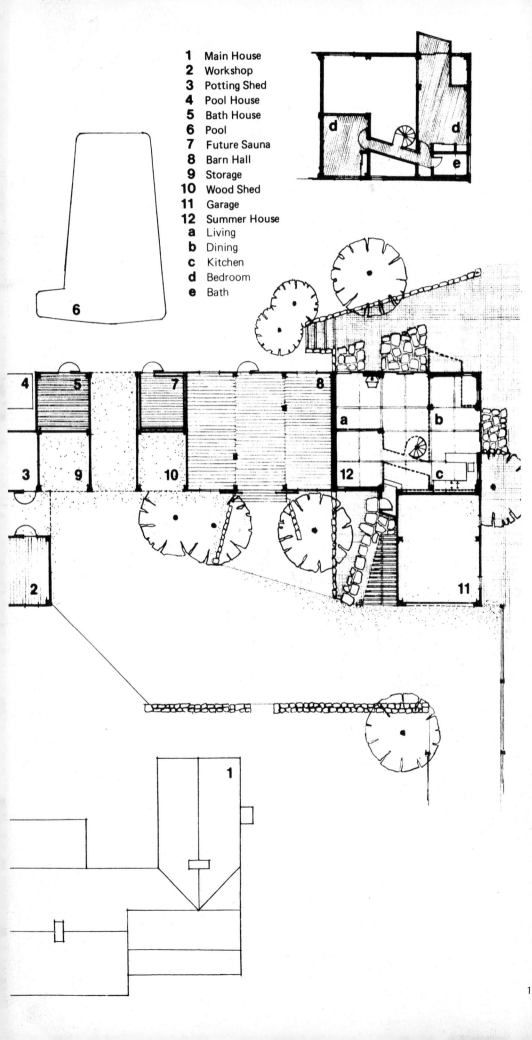

It was with a strong sense of history that architect Francis Booth transformed this historic Connecticut barn into a livable house for his family (3). For although the barn is contemporary, it never turns its back on the past. The summer house is built in one end of a long barn (2), with two small wings which form the sides of a courtyard (1). The fourth side is defined by an 18th-century farmhouse, in which a second family lives, and its outlying stone walls (3).

The structural elements of the existing barn were left in place and generated both the plan (1) and the elevations of the summer house. Thus, the living areas are reflective of the column spacing just as the window patterns express the beams and angled bracing in their configuration (5). The two-thirds of the barn not occupied by the summer house is left unfinished (4).

The courtyard (south) facade of the

3

5

barn has been left with a minimum of openings, the east face is broken by a series of small windows, and the north side has been opened up to fill the main space with light. A spiral staircase leads to two "bedroom houses," which are connected by a walkway (6, 7, 9, 10).

Old materials were used in the dining table and kitchen paneling, which were built out of oak and chestnut boards from the stall partitions and troughs. New materials include the concrete floor, the fir tongue-and-groove paneling for the bedroom houses, and the plasterboard with one coat of white sand finish for the walls and ceilings.

The summer house is heated solely by the fireplace (8). Since the farmhouse can be used in winter, other heat in the summer house was not provided; thus this section has not dried and shrunk away from the rest of the barn.

4

6

123

7

8

Much of the present pleasure of the house derives from the wit and skill of the contractor, whose understanding of the idea of a barn-house rather than a house-house was crucial to its realization.

The summer house and the farmhouse are actively used, and their physical relationship is paralleled by the social relationship of the two families who, while respecting each other's privacy, nonetheless share both the facility and obligations of the joint property.

9

10

The timbers and beams that form the basic structure for this house in Amenia, N.Y. (1), came from five old barns and cost only $200. The barns were slated to be bulldozed for site clearing in a park in upstate New York when architect Phil George purchased them from the state. The house now sits on a hill overlooking a valley 1,200 feet below.

Creating a barn from bits and pieces was not an easy job, recalls George, as people took home stray pieces of his five barns almost as fast as he could take them down. As a result, many of the joinings of the main timbers had to be fashioned over again by hand to fit properly. Pieces left over from the frames now form a sculpture in front of the house (2).

Inside, parts of other farm buildings have been re-used. The flooring is made of wide pine boards salvaged from the attic of a 1740s house, and the cabinets are made from siding.

The main living space soars 25 feet high to the top of the rafters, broken only by two cross-tie beams with diagonal struts which support a mid-roof purlin on each side (4). From the sleeping loft balcony, one sees the entire expanse of this space and the giant fieldstone fireplace at the far end (3).

1

2

3

4

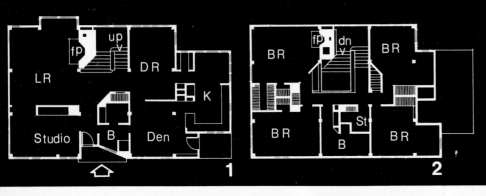

Architect Peter Jackson had this barn disassembled and moved 30 miles to its present location overlooking Long Island Sound. It was set on a new foundation and reassembled with the original vertical board siding (1, 2). The entire exterior was then covered with vertical cypress boards, exposing the original siding to the inside of the barn. Most other nonperimeter walls are sheetrock painted white, which emphasizes some of the structure and diagonal bracing of the original frame (3, 4).

One large rolling door as well as some interior doors were re-used from the original barn. While the romance of the old barn is essentially lost on the exterior, its presence is undeniable inside, even within the segmented spaces.

The architect and owners give much credit to the builder, Dennis Willmot, of Huntington, Vermont, who, with great concern for detail, mortised and tenoned and pegged the seemingly endless pieces of the giant puzzle.

1

2

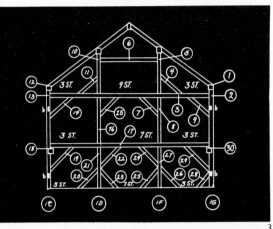

3

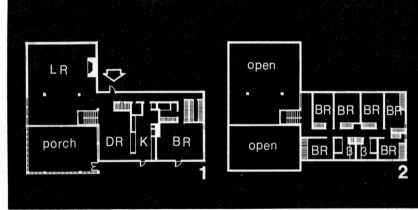

LR		
porch	DR	K	BR

1

open		BR	BR	BR	BR
open		BR	B	B	BR

2

4

Impelled by a longing for space, the Arthur Edelmans, a family with six children, in one grand gesture sold both their town house and a country cottage to buy an old barn, 30 acres of land, and a trout stream, in New England. The tottering barn turned out to be well worth the trouble involved in moving it beam by beam to its site next to the stream (1, 2). Each beam, carefully numbered and tagged (3), was reassembled with architect Charles Coiro directing a skillful carpenter.

Working closely with the architect, the owners acted as their own contractor. When slate was needed for the bathroom or tile for the floor, they delivered it themselves in the family station wagon. So that each child would have maximum privacy, the upper level was made into a six-bedroom, two-bath dormitory. As the house is subject to heavy traffic, durable materials were a priority. Concrete block interior walls and ceramic tile flooring provided the solution.

5

6

The great barn is divided into seasonal areas (4). In the summer it is open and cool with the screened-in porch as the main center of activity (7). The adjacent dining room can seat twelve comfortably. In winter the large living area (6, 8) is flooded with light and is very warm. Homesote panels on the ceiling are backed with an insulating material to make a protective layer under the slate roof (5).

7

8

In its original state this soft wine-red Connecticut barn already had the scale and charm of a rustic country residence (1). So architect Thomas J. Kupper had it moved from its original site piece by piece and re-erected. The original doors were replaced with large 20-pane windows. The sills were kept low to the ground. The floorboards from the original barn add a warmth to the interior finish, which highlights the original framing.

One of the nicest features is a small cozy dining room (3) whose windows open to the wooded side yard. The main access hall from kitchen to living room (4) is now lined with plants which thrive on the light from the three giant windows (2; also pp. 100–101). The second floor, containing bedrooms, is reached by a wide stairway. Designed originally for a family with eight children, the bedrooms are very spacious.

The present owner is Herbert D. Schutz.

When the co-owner of a construction company bought 60 acres in New Jersey for development, neighbors asked him to tear down a dilapidated early 1800s post-and-beam barn. Instead, he renovated it into a home for himself and his family (1).

Architect William Thomson saved everything possible — doors, flooring, beams — to be combined with new materials that had an old look. He was able to keep the stone foundation and most of the sheathing from the original barn. The most unusual feature of the exterior is in the handmade bricks that he used to fill in between the columns (2).

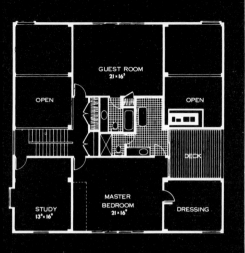

GUEST ROOM
21 × 16³

OPEN

OPEN

DECK

STUDY
13⁴ × 16⁶

MASTER
BEDROOM
21 × 16⁹

DRESSING

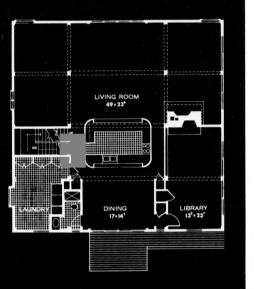

LIVING ROOM
49 × 23⁵

LAUNDRY

DINING
17 × 14⁵

LIBRARY
13⁵ × 23⁵

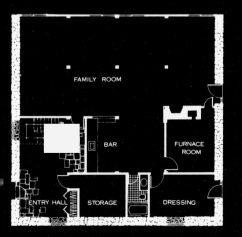

FAMILY ROOM

BAR

FURNACE
ROOM

ENTRY HALL

STORAGE

DRESSING

1

2

3

Transformation of this dairy barn (2, 3) into a New Jersey home (4) took only six months because the main structural frame had been left intact. Architects Short & Ford followed the lines of the existing structure with all new interior partitions (1). They also preserved an element that is one of the most unusual details in all barn design, the Dutch mortise, in which the mortised piece protrudes beyond the post (8). They have further accented the frame by using strong and bold colors on partition walls.

4

5

6

The lower floor, which opens out onto ground level at one end, has been transformed into a family room and bar. It has a small fireplace, which backs up to the furnace room. The chimney takes both flues. The main entry is on this level, where a staircase leads to the first floor. Here the kitchen has been built as a separate island element with the dining room beyond (6, 7). The dining room doors open on to a deck, which used to be the ramp access to the main threshing floor (5).

Above are bedrooms, which are completely enclosed from the main space for privacy, without, however, detracting from the cathedral ceiling effect on each side of the living room.

7

8

1

2

Architect Vincent Kling redesigned this stone barn near Kutztown, Pa., as a retreat and vacation house for a business group (1, 2).

The barn was later auctioned and inventor Ronald Penque bought it for his family's second home. He still uses the dining room and the fireplace, which are on the same level. The second level has a sort of wraparound living room with a balcony opening to the fireplace area below (3). The top level contains bedrooms which are enclosed from the main space. All levels are reached by one spiral staircase (4). The natural colors of the materials — warm gray barn timbers, soft-hued limestone, and dark-stained wood floors — are all enhanced by the natural sunlight coming through the east window wall (5).

5

4

1

2

3

Architect Tim Prentice had already completed several barn renovations when he began this project in Connecticut. From the road, the original exterior (1) gives little hint that this barn is now a home. Even when the two large doors are open, all that one sees is the old barn floor (now used as a recreation area). One hardly suspects what is beyond it.

On the other side Prentice has dramatically changed the barn's exterior with new triangular glazed areas and new roof lines (3). On the far end he has opened up the entire end wall to a view of the farm pond and the woods beyond.

Inside he has used slick white ceiling surfaces to reflect the light into each part of the room (2, 4). The second-story bedrooms are reached either from the front or the rear.

4

1

2

3

4

5

6

The basic gable shape with a lean-to at the side is typical of many Long Island barns. This austere form was almost reason enough to undertake the rescue of this barn (1). For architects Julian and Barbara Neski and owner Edward Dent, an advertising executive, it was important to keep the shape of the barn intact in the remodeling (4).

Sheathed in plywood, the building was first moved several feet (2, 3). The original weathered cedar shingles and white trim were re-used and add to the strong simplicity of the exterior. Rolling barn door shutters protect the glass areas from the elements when the house is closed up.

Throughout, the modernization was handled with restraint. The original structural system was left intact,

135

7

8

open		E
BR		LR
St		K
		BR	B	BR

and the textures of the roof and beams serve as the main form of enrichment of the interior (5). Sand-finish plaster was applied to the walls, and the entire living room floor was covered with Mexican tiles. The floor was kept near the existing grade; sliding glass doors floor to eaves recall the long, low expanse of the once-farmed potato fields of Long Island.

The interior is filled with light even on an overcast day, so that the dark ceiling mass accentuates the space of the main area. A small balcony bedroom is reached by a spiral staircase, which is seen from the kitchen (6). Looking over this balcony one can see the fireplace and free-standing chimney flue (7–10).

9

10

This complex near East Hampton includes an L-shaped assortment of old outbuildings and an old wood frame house (1, 2). The barn and another building were moved intact by truck and placed adjacent to the house. Architect Donald Ritchey, with Carl Warns, renovated the house for artist Arthur Williams.

The effect of the main interior space is based on a contrast between slick white surfaces and the exposed rough main structural timbers of the original barn. To further emphasize this contrast, the floor is covered with small white ceramic tiles. Light literally filters through the entire space. The design is one of utmost austere simplicity, which highlights the decorative sculptural objects in the room (3, 5).

The largest single element of the complex is the barn, which has been designed as a pool house with an open cathedral ceiling (4). The walls were sprayed with urethane foam for insulation and soundproofing. Above the pool will be the owner's painting studio. Here, and in other parts of the house, walls have been opened to the woods through generous glass areas.

5

1

In the Connecticut countryside is this small 1720 barn remodeled by architect Philip Johnson. Originally, it was a typical cow barn with hay storage above and stalls below.

What Johnson accomplished was to transform what must have been a dark interior into one filled with sunlight. He opened one entire wall with glass (1). To continue the effect at night he directed lights on the eaves above the glass wall toward the porch below. He took the classical-looking frame on the end wall and emphasized it by placing stark white plaster between the members. At each end of the barn is a new fireplace laid up with a rubble-type fieldstone (2). From outside, the entire skeletal framework of the barn can be seen. From inside, the surrounding wooded countryside is visible.

2

1

2

This remodeled carriage house in Illinois has always been a building to provoke admiration. In 1895, the grandfather of present owner Edward H. Bennett, Jr., commissioned architect Henry Ives Cobb to design a carriage house and dairy barn as aesthetically distinguished as the family residence on the Bennett estate. This structure of classic proportions was the result (1).

Sixty-five years later the grandson, an architect himself, had reacquired the family heirloom. He retained the still substantial and beautiful shell, but completely reapportioned the building's vast interior space into this serene dwelling for his family of six. He made the foyer a light-washed gallery for the display of art (2) and turned the carriage room into a museum for his antique cars.

Interior remodeling was extensive — the equivalent of building an en-

tirely new, very contemporary house — but the exterior retains its original classic dignity. The drama of the plan is provided by the staircase, which rises from the entry foyer to the gabled living room, originally the hayloft (3). The living room surrounds the stairwell, thus appearing to be several rooms. The old half-moon windows and the barn posts and beams are treated as major decoration, giving a pavilionlike quality.

3

This barn in Bridgehampton, N.Y., doubles as a second home and some-time studio for painter Manoucher Yektai (1). To achieve maximum space and control of light, he and Richard Kaplan came up with an open, workable plan. The ceiling is lowered over the entry to reduce the scale of the interior (2). Then the space soars to the rafters in the main living area (3).

Yektai wanted movement and this thinking was applied to the design of the stone fireplace as well. Rather than have the mason carefully cut and fit each stone, Yektai asked him simply to lay them up in a natural fashion. At first the mason resisted, but after completing the job, he liked it so well that he has specialized in this method of stonework ever since.

1

Despite its contemporary exterior (1), this nearly 250-year-old Long Island barn has the dignity of old age and weathered wood. When architect Richard Kaplan, an ardent conservationist, found the structure, he decided to keep as many of the beams and rafters as possible. The shingles from the exterior were re-used inside on the entry wall (2), while paneling was obtained from a 150-year-old barn in Maine. The floor boards are pine stained dark. An antique table serves as the bar, and above it are old shuttered panels (3). Behind these panels is the kitchen, which has a ceiling open to the main area. High berms and earth banks surround the property, making the small lot private. The earth for these berms was taken from the pool excavation.

2

3

1

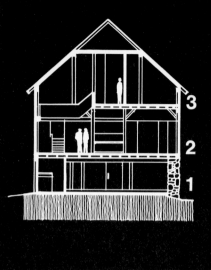

4

Typical of many dairy barns, this one in Ithaca, N.Y., was built into a hillside, resulting in a natural stone retaining wall on the lower level (1). The new owners, a young couple, wanted to convert it into modest living quarters. They planned to retain the character and integrity of the old barn and to allow for future conversion as their family grew (4).

They had William Schickel undertake the renovation, a designer whose

2

3

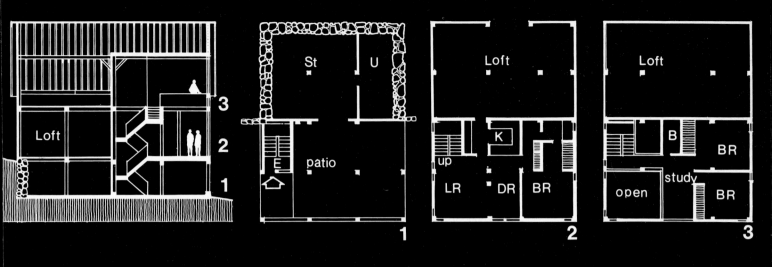

work exhibits an interesting Shaker simplicity. The original framework and stonework were preserved as much as possible (2, 3). It was decided at the outset that new work should look new and the existing structure should look old (5, 6). New windows follow the original pattern of narrow slots, which further dramatizes the height of the interior space.

5

6

143

1

When architect Robert Felson began renovation on this 100-year-old barn in Yorktown Heights, N.Y., he decided to leave it on its site and to leave the original siding intact (1).

The maximum amount of light, required by the owners, gives this structure its contemporary look. The large window areas (2) are the most dramatic change from barn into residence.

Inside, the heavy hand-hewn timbers are left intact and exposed. They were treated with a preservative to enhance their natural color. Natural-colored plaster was used on the interior walls, giving them a rough-textured finish that complements the warm tone of the timbers.

The stairway was constructed of new heavy timbers to blend in with the other wood members (3). Recessed light for the stairs was installed underneath the handrails.

3

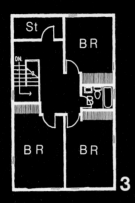

3

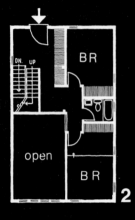

2

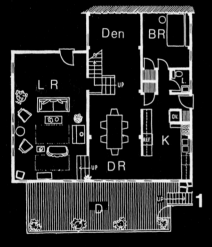

1

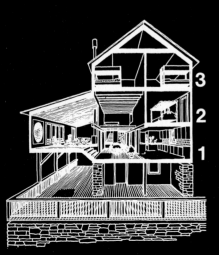

THE JOHNSTON HAR_STER CO.
FARM MACHINERY.

3

During its lifespan, this 150-year-old former grist mill has twice been the victim of fires. When the present owners, who use it as a Connecticut weekend retreat, discovered it several years ago, it had been abandoned for over 20 years and vandalized. Nothing remained but a shell. Architect Tim Prentice received an architectural award of merit for his rejuvenation of it (1, preceding page).

The exterior framework and finish were in good condition and only a few clapboards had to be replaced. New windows were installed, selected for slimness to exaggerate their height and conform with the verticality of the tall building. The tin roof was also usable and needed but a coat of paint to protect it.

Since the mill had been used more as a warehouse consisting of very large areas, the major portion of the remodeling concentrated on the interiors. In tackling them, Prentice insisted that the various floor levels be maintained to clearly define living areas.

The interior materials were chosen for simplicity and ease of maintenance. Walls are drywall and the floors in the kitchen and bathroom are quarry tile. The original structural beams were left intact and exposed wherever possible to contrast with the white painted walls (3).

A section through the building shows the levels with the new lower terrace overlooking a fast-running stream (2).

This restored barn and house sit on 150 acres of land with two streams in West Hebron, N.Y. (1). They are part of a group of buildings that were so run down they didn't cost anything — two barns, ramshackle farmhouse, and chicken coop. But the stone foundations of the 1820 barn were sound, and there were beautiful hand-hewn beams along with the slate and chestnut floorboards.

Architect Charles Mount and author Daniel Rosenblatt wanted to update the concept and function of all the spaces. In the house this meant opening up an atrium that rises 23 feet in the middle of the main area (2). The ground floor is used as a wine cellar. On the second floor are four bedrooms which are joined by a 40-foot-long catwalk made from aluminum subway grating (3). A circular wrought iron staircase connects all three floors (4).

Architect Mount has planned many barn renovations for others, but this one is all his own. At entry level is a large kitchen. In the upper-level studio and large bedroom, also connected by a catwalk, he has

whitewashed the entire interior, including the beams (5). The furniture is small in scale to further emphasize the openness and height of the rooms. Except for a simple contemporary cube — the platform beds and shelves — the furnishings are all local finds, picked up at auctions and fairs (6).

4

5

3

6

This great stone barn in northern Virginia (1) predates the Civil War, and there are legends that it was used as a Confederate hospital. It is tremendous in size, measuring 40 by 80 feet and consisting of five bays.

In renovating this weekend residence, architects Wilkes & Faulkner Associates at first used only two bays for the living area and left the rest in its natural state (2). Later the owners decided to utilize two more bays for a basketball court and game room. A new plywood floor was installed over the existing giant round timbers in the floor, some as large as 24 inches across. The main timber across the floor is a 14-by-20-inch hand-hewn beam 40 feet long.

Inside the main space (3, 4) the architects have used both old barn siding and sand-finish plaster for the walls. The ceiling has been sprayed with urethane foam and spray painted white.

The original barn faced an old farmhouse, but the new owners have changed the orientation to the opposite side, where they get a 60-mile view of the Blue Ridge Mountains and enjoy spectacular sunsets.

CHAPTER 10
Barn Art

Once the hay and livestock are gone, an old barn becomes a challenging place. When tackled by spirited clients and responsive architects, it often ceases to recall its original function. Modified by new openings or wings located and shaped with deliberate aesthetic intent, it sets forth the life-styles of its new inhabitants and is a barn no more. As in the projects on the following pages, its form will still be apparent, but its life and function will have been transformed.

Designed and built by graduate architecture students from Yale, this barn for Alan and Jill Bomser began in 1968 when student Tom Platt responded to an ad to renovate a barn. What followed was a year of design and construction that produced one of the most unusual and experimental barn remodelings ever.

The 100-year-old barn stands on a winding dirt road in the Hudson Valley in upstate New York (1). Its battered tin roof was bent back, revealing the old rafters.

In the main area, which is 30 feet from floor to ridge, are the great hall and dining room. A few feet up from the main floor is the living room (4), where a used-brick fireplace displays an arched opening which relates to the circular openings in the bedroom spaces above.

To accommodate the bedrooms (2), the gabled barn was given two upper galleries, joined by a bridge. In the center is a large well open to the roof, which is visible through the arched openings, the circles counterpointing the strong, straight lines of the barn (3). The pie-shaped flaps pull up to enclose the bedrooms.

All the old existing parts of the barn were left rough and textured and all the new materials are smooth, crisply modern, and highly colorful. The overall concept is of space rearranged and fragmented in such a way as to give this renovation a sense of structured order.

The original three-part interior demarcation of this large carriage house in Bedford, N.Y., was carried over as the basis for the new living zones (1, 2). Architect Myron Goldfinger skillfully transformed the spaces to include the best from two eras, contemporary simplicity set against details preserved from the past. The central garage became an enormous living-dining room (4) and the stable at one end was turned into a sizable art gallery for the owner. What used to be the chauffeur's quarters is now a study-library downstairs with three guest bedrooms above.

The second floor above the gallery is a large master bedroom suite where the original beams and diagonal bracing are left exposed (3).

1

2

3

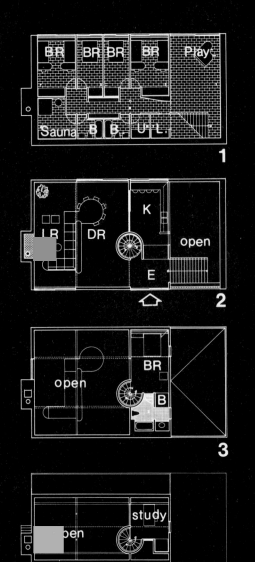

1

2

3

4

2

3

In architect Charles Gwathmey's design for this barn-into-residence project in Greenwich, Conn., he chose to work exclusively with the interior volumes (1). What he accomplished was to diminish visually the scale of the exterior while magnifying the sense of space on the interior. The entry door, for instance, is overscaled to make the building look smaller (2).

Service and circulation spaces were designed on one side of the structure and living spaces on the other (4). Each area was referenced to the main center line of the roof ridge. A photo mural covering the entire

4

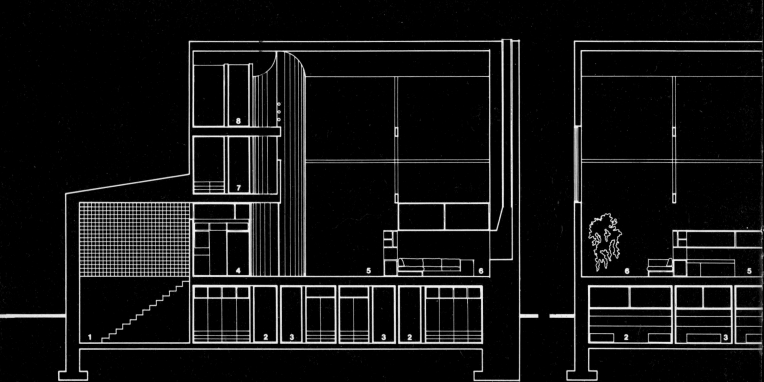

end wall of the playroom on the lower level serves to relate the main entry level to the one below (3).

The cabinetwork is designed to modulate the spaces on the lower level. They are of white oak, while the interior is double-layered sheet-rock painted throughout. The round end of the large, custom-made dining table echoes the design of the spiral staircase (5).

The master bedroom and study levels are intended to be a separate building within the large volume with views to the exterior and views over-looking the main space (6, 7).

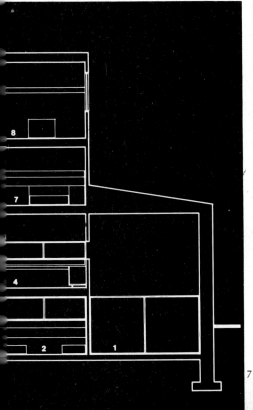

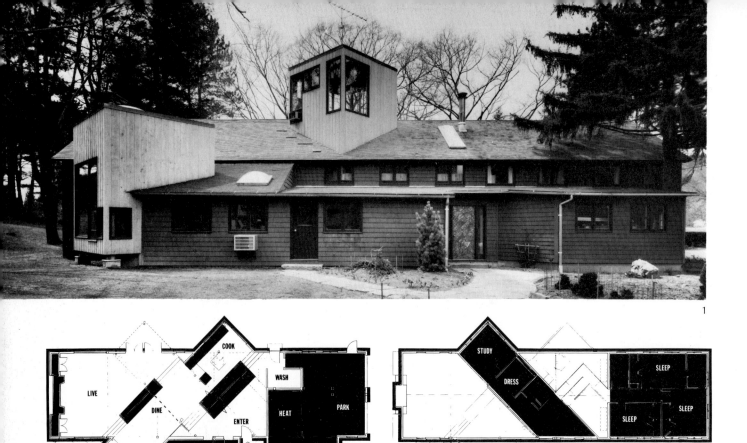

1

2

There is a deliberate and unmistakable contract between old and new in this Connecticut barn-to-house renovation for a family of five by Hardy Holzman Pfeiffer (1).

The structure makes use of three new cubelike rooms, aligned diagonally to the original structure (2). The window areas in the cubes let light into three major spaces: the kitchen, study, and a solarium-greenhouse (3, 4).

All surfaces, both exterior and interior, were completely resurfaced with materials that emphasize the old and the new. The old shingles are dark brown and the new forms are light colored, rough-sawn boards. On the interior the existing dark, heavy timbers are contrasted with Mexican tile floors and with stark white sheetrock for walls and ceilings (5, 6).

3

4

5

6

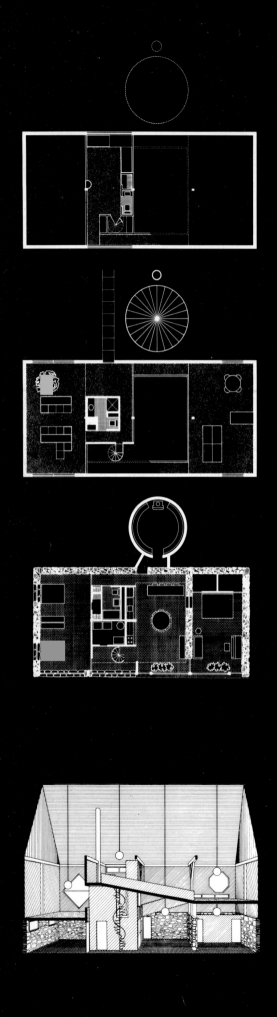

2

4

The owners of this barn wanted to build a big open summer house on their 200 acres of fields and woods in southern Wisconsin. They didn't consider their barn until their architect, Stanley Tigerman, came out to the farm and convinced them to convert it.

A local carpenter was hired to effect the plan. The design calls for an open plan with all elements left exposed (1). The exterior envelope was completely remade (2), after which the electrical system was put in with exposed conduits, switch plates, and receptacles, all color coded. The plumbing and ductwork are also exposed and color coded. Rough-sawn cedar siding was placed diagonally inside and out (4, 5). This not only strengthens the structure but sets off the original framework and stone. The silo foundation was left in its original state and made into a study (3).

3

5

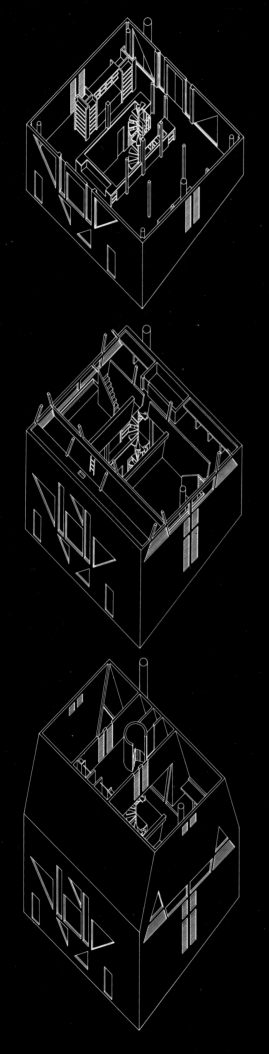

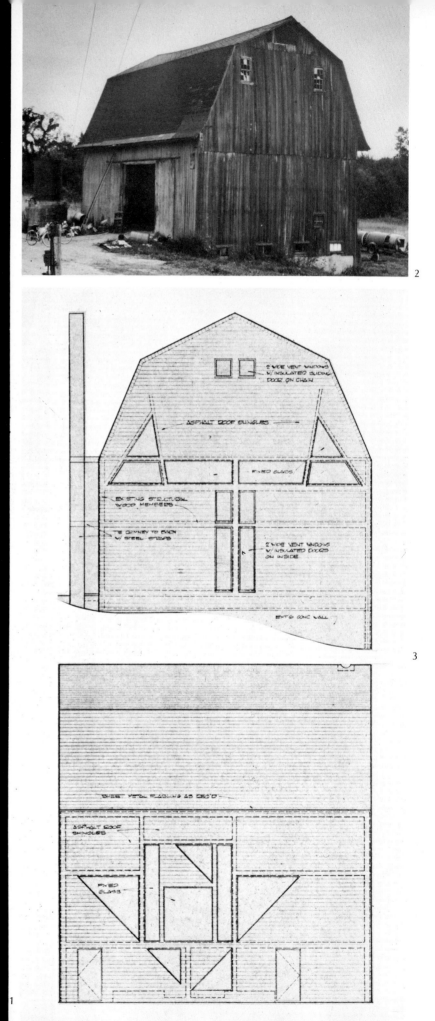

1

2

3

When veterinarian Jim Christiansen looked for a site for his house, he wanted it in the country. He therefore purchased a 130-acre apple orchard called Frog Hollow, in Wisconsin. The Pennsylvania Dutch, who had settled there a century ago, had built a big barn with log columns, hand-hewn beams, and overhead a mansard roof which had partially collapsed (2). To the Christiansens, the idea of a barn-house precisely matched their ideas about living. They like openness and they have a nostalgia for haylofts, both having been brought up on farms.

The Christiansens hired architect Stanley Tigerman to remodel this 19th-century relic. They asked him to provide areas for living together and for being alone. Mrs. Christiansen needed space and light for her painting, and room had to be made for a large pipe organ. This led Tigerman to conceive of the barn as a multidimensional container, accommodating many activities inside (1, 3). Preserving the timbers and beams, he infilled them with rough-finished red cedar. This not only enhances them but provides structural stiffening. The roof overhangs were trimmed off, and the exterior was then totally sheathed in plywood and covered top to bottom with black asphalt shingles (6).

Adding to the monolithic, sculptural effect are clusters of windows of gray-tinted glass in the shape of triangles, squares, rectangles, and trapezoids. The placement of these graphic windows, which appear semi-opaque from the outside, was partially determined by existing beams.

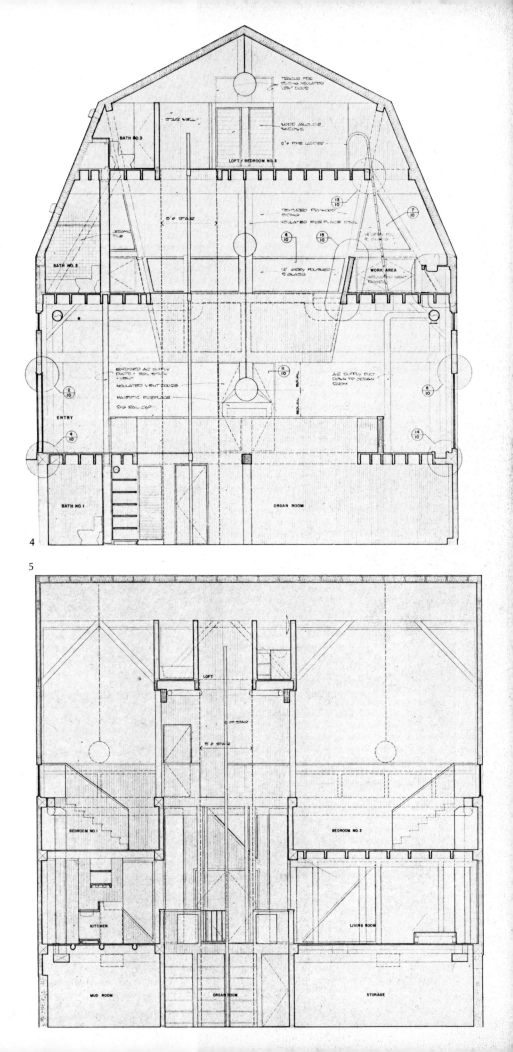

6

The four levels of living are linked by a spiral staircase, which becomes a sculptural focal point (7, 8). The sections illustrated show how they relate to the existing hand-hewn frame (4, 5). On the lowest level are the organ and storage rooms. The second level contains the kitchen, dining, and living rooms, all surrounding the open central well. The next level contains the children's bedrooms, baths, and the combination bridge and painting studio. On the top level are the master bedroom and master bath.

The total effect of the use of materials inside and out is one of simplicity. The asphalt-shingled exterior is not only practical and economical, but dramatic. Inside, the untreated red cedar textured paneling is an effective contrast to the exterior. The entire interior surface reflects light from the large window areas to all parts of the structure. The bright primary color-coded conduits, heating ducts, and plumbing are exposed and all carefully threaded through the structure. Although this feature was basically an economy measure, it provides a colorful relief and accent to the interior wood paneling.

7

8

CHAPTER 11
New Homes from Barn Profiles

It has been said by many architects that the barn as a building type may well represent America's highest architectural achievement. It is no surprise, then, that the barn profile has shown up in many contemporary structures. Sometimes the similarities are intentional but more often they are unconscious reflections of forms that are strongly rooted in the past. This heritage is often displayed with great strength, as in the following projects.

The barn-home is fast gaining in popularity, not only in the re-use of old barns, but in new buildings using modern technology, such as prefabrication. The barn was America's earliest prefabricated structure and is once again a way to build a barn. Although the prefabricated market has a second-class reputation, it has nevertheless become the building mode of the present and future.

The first stage in the design of a prefabricated barn-home is the construction of a scale model (1) of the frame, outlining the exact number and placement of each piece of the basic structural frame. There are several basic types and, of course, there are endless variations that can be adapted from the basic frame shape.

Barn Homes, based in Woodstock, N.Y., is one of several companies that build prefabricated barn frames. It takes a certain amount of modernized manufacturing to prepare the rough-sawn large timbers for the frames (2). These timbers are then fashioned with mortise-and-tenon joints so that they can be pegged together at the site (3, 5). Here is where modern techniques leave off and fusion with past principles of building begins.

The frames are joined together on the ground- or first-floor platform (4, 6). The jointing is secured with the old wooden beetle used by barn erectors a century ago and, as in a barn

8

9

10

raising bee, the frames are lifted into place (by crews supplied by Barn Homes) (7–10). Once the frame is upright the top tie beams are mounted onto the tenoned posts and the roof rafters are added (11). The finished product looks exactly like the early design model before the prefabricated roof and wall panels are installed (12).

12

11

Barn Homes offers the skilled or unskilled do-it-yourself homesteader an inexpensive structure. The frame is fashioned from simple, tried-and-true building principles. The post-and-beam construction makes the placement of interior walls extremely flexible (15, 16). They can be adapted to many different requirements, whether left completely open or enclosed to make smaller rooms.

The founder and owner of the company, Dominique Storm van Leeuwen, who lives in a century-old barn which he is remodeling, has imparted some of the strength, beauty in simplicity, and endurance of old barns to the Barn Homes structure. The wide range of interior treatments possible makes it a versatile alternative to the typical tract split-level home with cathedral ceilings (13, 14, 17–22).

17

18

19

20

21

22

1

Shown on this page is a strongly angular house that, with its fresh shingles, looks new (1). It is not. The main section is a small house built in the 1920s, and the wing is an 1812 barn moved from an adjacent property. The barn was used for horses until a few days before it was dismantled, moved, reconstructed, and remodeled by architect Eugene Futterman. It stands among acres of farmland in Sagaponac, Long Island.

Since this first joining of barn and house, Futterman has sharpened his

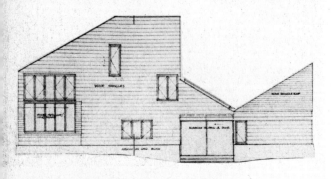

2

3

concern for the inherent style and strength of the classic barn in other Long Island projects (2, 3). Having grown tired of the ever-present International Style vacation homes that dot the beach frontage in Eastern Long Island, he has developed a style that is more indigenous to the area, to the low-lying potato fields, and to the local barn vernacular. It reached its height in the design of his own home in the same area, pictured here in elevation and under construction (4–6). The main structural forms of his houses are enhanced by angular sheds and changing roof lines and by openings carved out to emphasize these shapes. These structures are strongly influenced by barn forms, yet they still have a character and vitality of their own.

This same concern for simplicity of form is expressed in the two contemporary designs opposite. 7. A residence in Connecticut by architects Markisz & Magnani, New York. 8. An award-winning design on Long Island by Ed Copeland, Architect.

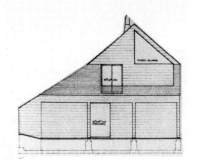

4

5

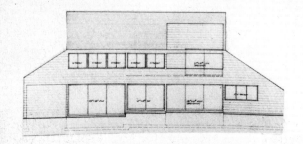

6

7

8

173

1

Because most farm buildings were much larger than residences, the contemporary form that relates most closely to the scale of the barn is the multiresidential structure. Brook Hollow in Hanover, N.H., is a good example of how New England vernacular architecture has made its way into contemporary design (1–6). Designed by architects Day and Ertman for Levitt Residential Communities, it provides not only a barnlike architectural profile but a human scale by the extension of the roof lines to form shedlike entryways.

2

3

All across America, farmland is rapidly disappearing and new structures are being built. Seeing barns designed by carpenters side by side with contemporary buildings clarifies the fundamental similarities between them.

In Hunter, N.Y., the Scribner Hollow project includes town houses, motor lodge, and restaurant (2). It is immediately adjacent to farm property with an old horse barn as a reminder of the past (1).

On the northern California coast lies Sea Ranch, one of the most renowned condominium developments of the day (3). The buildings relate well to the coastline, the cliffs, and the gently sloping foothills. They also express the strength and simplicity of form of the California barn.

On reclaimed farmland in Roxbury, N.Y., is a condominium development, Roxbury Run, whose large, three-story structure recalls the farming heritage of the area (4).

1

2

4

This building is not a renovated barn, nor did architect Louis Mackall have a barn form in mind when he designed this home on Nantucket for a client. He wanted a large and simple shape with openings that varied from very large to very small, interior space that was grand but certainly not grandiose, a structure that was primarily a shelter and not a piece of modern exhibitionism. In short, he wanted the simple, forthright expression of space and form that barns seem to have naturally because they have escaped architectural classification and have not been subject to endless watered-down copying.

In this house, the architect was totally involved in the carrying out of his design. As a cabinetmaker, he supplied and installed all the special woodwork and skylights for the entire job.

Bibliography

HISTORY

Arthur, Eric, and Dudley Witney. *The Barn: A Vanishing Landmark*. Greenwich, Conn.: New York Graphic Society, 1972. In this lavish pictorial record of North American barns, the authors examine many barns externally and internally from the perspectives of architect and photographer.

Ball, Berenice M. *Barns of Chester County, Pennsylvania*. West Chester, Pa.: The Chester County Day Committee of the Women's Auxiliary, 1974. Treats Chester County barns old and new, with photographs dating from the 1800s to the present, and with special chapters on such subjects as adaptive uses and stories of local barns.

Barn Plans and Outbuildings. New York: Orange Judd, 1904. Practical advice is given to farmers of the early 1900s on the construction of barns and farm buildings and on the housing and care of livestock.

Fitchen, John. *The New World Dutch Barn*. Syracuse, N.Y.: Syracuse University Press, 1968. A technical description of early American barns, including an analysis of the structural systems and the probable building procedures followed.

Glassie, Henry. *Barn Building in Otsego County, New York*. Bloomington, Ind.: Folklore Institute, Indiana University, 1974. This geographical survey of barn architecture in a New York county carefully examines barn types that typify barn construction over a wider geographical area and chronological period.

Lassiter, William Lawrence. *Shaker Architecture*. New York: Bonanza, 1966. Treats Shaker architecture and the people who created it; generous use of cross-sections and floor plans.

Pennsylvania German Barns. Allentown, Pa.: The Pennsylvania German Folklore Society, 1958. The history and design of Pennsylvania German barns, with detailed descriptions and photographs of eleven specific buildings.

Rudofsky, Bernard. *Architecture Without Architects*. New York: Museum of Modern Art, 1962.

Sloane, Eric. *An Age of Barns*. New York: Funk & Wagnalls, n.d. In this superbly illustrated history, author-artist Sloane uses pen-and-ink drawings to examine early barns and building techniques.

———. *American Barns and Covered Bridges*. New York: Funk & Wagnalls, 1954. Early American barns and covered bridges along with many of the tools crafted for building purposes are illustrated and examined.

———. *I Remember America*. New York: Funk & Wagnalls, 1971. With reminiscences and talk of country things by Sloane, the chapters wander warmly via paintings, drawings, and prose over marshes, roads, barns, and covered bridges.

———. *A Reverence for Wood*. New York: Ballantine, 1974. Pen-and-ink illustrations, combined with early American lore, explore the application of native woods to building, making utensils and containers, and producing charcoal.

Shoemaker, Alfred L. *The Pennsylvania Barn*. Lancaster, Pa.: Franklin Dutch Folklore Center, 1955.

Thollander, Earl. *Barns of California*. San Francisco: California Historical Society, 1974. This collection of drawings with delightful descriptive notes includes barns and distinctive rural buildings throughout California.

RESTORATION

Boericke, Art, and Barry Shapiro. *Handmade Houses: A Guide to the Woodbutcher's Art*. San Francisco: Scrimshaw, 1973. A record with color photographs of unique and memorable owner-built structures, many built from salvaged materials.

Bruyere, Christian, and Robert Inwood. *In Harmony with Nature: Creative Country Construction*. New York: Drake, 1975. Two former apartment-dwellers share their acquired homesteading expertise in subjects ranging from drainage systems and root cellars to complete construction of a home.

Cantacuzino, Sherban. *New Uses for Old Buildings*. New York: Watson-Guptill, 1975. International examples of major conversions of barns, churches, and warehouses are included with the history, character, and technical problems unique to each restoration.

Fracchia, Charles A., and Jeremiah O. Bragstad. *Converted into Houses*. New York: Viking, 1976. Colorful survey of conversions of many building types, including barns, factories, schools, firehouses, and ferryboats.

House & Garden Book of Modern Houses and Conversions. London: Conde Nast, 1966. Approximately 100 new houses and 50 conversions in the U.S.A. and Europe are included with photographs and plans. Projects range from a treetop house in California to a converted stable in Denmark.

Kinney, Jean and Cle. *47 Creative Homes That Started as Bargain Buildings.* New York: Funk & Wagnalls, 1974. Photographs, floor plans, drawings, and charts help chronicle the conversions of forty-seven homes that began as barns, outbuildings, and other bargain purchases.

Klamkin, Charles. *Barns: Their History, Preservation, and Restoration.* New York: Hawthorn, 1973. This photographic essay recounts early American barn-building techniques along with a plea to "save the barns."

Matson, Peter H. *A Place in the Country.* New York: Random House, 1977. Personal story of a barn rebuilding that rambles through such topics as the actual work involved, the high cost of materials, seeking cheap labor, and encounters with local folk and fauna.

Shelter. Bolinas, Calif.: Shelter Publications, 1973. A study of simple homes built by resourceful men and societies around the globe, extensively illustrated.

Stanforth, Deirdre. *Restored America.* New York: Praeger, 1975. Two-thirds of the book is devoted to photographs and descriptions of fine old houses across the country that have been restored, the other third to adaptive uses made of such old buildings as warehouses, factories, barns, and theaters.

Thompson, Elizabeth Kendall, ed. *Recycling Buildings: Renovations, Remodelings, Restorations, and Reuses.* New York: McGraw-Hill, 1977. Major projects by architects, covering many building types across the U.S.A.; compiled from the pages of *Architectural Record.*

REFERENCE AND HOW-TO

Cole, John, and Charles Wing. *From the Ground Up: The Shelter Institute Guide to Building Your Own House.* Boston: Atlantic–Little, Brown, 1976.

Doyle, John M. *The Complete Home Owner's Guide.* Reston, Va.: Reston Publishing Company, 1975. For the potential homeowner, this guide provides information on architectural types of homes, what to look for and look out for when househunting, and practical advice covering legal questions, mortgages, maintenance, plumbing, and electricity.

Elliott, Stewart, and Eugenie Wallas. *The Timber Framing Book.* York, Maine: Housesmiths Press, 1976. Many drawings, details, and photographs illustrate how to construct a timber frame house step by step.

Price, Irving. *Buying Country Property: Pitfalls and Pleasures.* New York: Harper & Row, 1972. A real estate expert covers property taxes, zoning, water supply, lake property, and subdivisions.

Robinson, David. *The Complete Homesteading Book.* Charlotte, Vt.: Garden Way, 1974. This basic guide book for the homesteader gives advice on buying land, planning and building the homestead, utility systems, and raising food and animals.

Young, Jean and Jim. *People's Guide to Country Real Estate.* New York: Praeger, 1973. Practical advice for the beginner on finding and purchasing country land and buildings, choosing a bank and a lawyer, and other aspects of ownership such as remodeling, insurance, contracts, and appraisals.

Credits

DESIGN CREDITS

page no.

44, 45   Beard Residence, Montauk Point, N.Y.
         Peter Beard
         Montauk Point, N.Y.

50   Britt Residence and Studio, Cary, N.C.
         William M. Britt, Architect
         Raleigh, N.C.

51   Office and Pool House, Franklin, Tenn.
         Orr/Houk & Associates Architects Inc.
         Nashville, Tenn.

52   Office Project, Madison, Wis.
         Homer Fieldhouse, Feldhausen Associates
         Madison, Wis.

53   Hoftyzer Residence, Otsego County, N.Y.
         Peter Hoftyzer
         Brooklyn, N.Y.

54   Residence, Brewster, N.Y.
         David Glasser, Glasser and Ohlhausen
         New York, N.Y.

55   Residence, Massachusetts
         Juster Pope Associates, Architects and Planners
         Shelburn Falls, Mass.

56, 57   Residence, New Canaan, Conn.
         Howard A. Patterson, Jr., Architect
         Darien, Conn.

58–69   Burden Residence, Hunter Mountain, N.Y.
         Ernest Burden, Architect
         New York, N.Y.

70, 71   Storm van Leeuwen Residence, Woodstock,
         N.Y.
         Dominique Storm van Leeuwen
         Woodstock, N.Y.

72, 73   Bell Residence, Accord, N.Y.
         James Byron Bell Associates, Architects
         New York, N.Y.

78, 79   Borderline Farm, Enosburg Falls, Vt.
         Moritz O. Bergmeyer, Architect
         Boston, Mass.

80, 81   Lucerne Shopping Center, Ballwin, Mo.
         Jay Reiter
         St. Louis, Mo.

82, 83   Sheraton Motor Inn, Fredericksburg, Va.
         Edward F. Sinnott & Son, Architects
         Richmond, Va.

84   Oliver's Carriage House, Columbia, Md.
         Lang Design/Research Inc.
         Columbia, Md.

85   Casagmo Recreation Center, Plainfield, Conn.
         Lee Harris Pomeroy, Architect
         New York, N.Y.

86, 87   Offices, New Paltz and Liberty, N.Y.
         Liebman and Hurwitz, Architects & Planners
         New Paltz, N.Y.

88, 89   Office, Imlaystown, N.J.
         Zion & Breen Associates, Landscape Architects
         Imlaystown, N.J.

90, 91   Darrow School, Lebanon, N.Y.
         Dairy Barn: Llewelyn-Davies, New York, N.Y.
         Science Building: George Lewis, James Baker,
         Llewelyn-Davies, New York, N.Y.

92   Visual Arts Center, Maryland
         Lang Design/Research Inc.
         Columbia, Md.

93   Greenwich Art Barn, Greenwich, Conn.
         Thomas J. Kupper, Architect
         Greenwich, Conn.

94, 95   Blenheim-Gilboa Pumped Storage Power
         Project
         Paul Malo, Professor of Architecture
         Syracuse University, Syracuse, N.Y.

96   Simon's Rock Art Center, Great Barrington,
         Mass.
         Hardy Holzman Pfeiffer Associates
         New York, N.Y.

97   Taylor Theater, Lockport, N.Y.
         Hardy Holzman Pfeiffer Associates
         New York, N.Y.

98   Grailville Oratory, Loveland, Ohio
         Schickel Design & Development Co.
         Ithaca, N.Y.
         Collaborating architect:
         Garber Tweddle & Wheeler
         Cincinnati, Ohio

99   Chain O'Lakes Covenant Church, McHenry, Ill.
         Rowe, Abplanalp & Johnson, Architects
         Park Ridge, Ill.

104–106 Residences
         Richard Babcock
         Hancock, Mass.

105 (7-9)   *Stern Residence,* Hancock, Mass.
            William Hammer, Architect
            Lexington, Mass.

107-108   *Hofmann Residence/Studio,* Catskill
            Mountains, N.Y.
            Natalia Pohrebynsky

109   *Mason Residence/Studio,* Long Island, N.Y.
            Richard Schust, Architect
            East Hampton, N.Y.

110 (top)   *Office/Residence,* Riegelsville, Pa.
            William Callahan, Architect
            Donald Sarstedt, Sarstedt & Associates,
            Designer
            Riegelsville, Pa.

110 (bottom) *Beadle Residence,* East Hampton, N.Y.
            Gina Beadle
            East Hampton, N.Y.

111, 112   *Rolland Residence,* Copes Bridge, Pa.
            William Rolland
            West Chester, Pa.

113   *Heimann Residence,* East Hampton, N.Y.
            Richard Heimann
            East Hampton, N.Y.

116, 117   *Residence,* Napa Valley, Calif.
            William Weber Kirsch, Architect
            Sausalito, Calif.

118, 119   *Residences,* Ashfield and Conway, Mass.
            Juster Pope Associates, Architects and Planners
            Shelburn Falls, Mass.

120, 121   *Cullins Residence,* Charlotte, Vt.
            Thomas V. S. Cullins, Architect
            Burlington, Vt.

122-124   *Booth Residence,* Connecticut
            Francis Booth, Architect
            New York, N.Y.

125   *George Residence,* Amenia, N.Y.
            Phil George, Harper and George, Architects
            New York, N.Y.

126   *Residence,* Long Island, N.Y.
            Peter Jackson, Architect
            Branford, Conn.

127, 128   *Edelman Residence,* Ridgefield, Conn.
            Charles Coiro, Architect
            Ridgefield, Conn.

129   *Schutz Residence,* Greenwich, Conn.
            Thomas J. Kupper, Architect
            Greenwich, Conn.

130   *Residence,* Princeton, N.J.
            William M. Thomson, Architect
            Princeton, N.J.

131, 132   *Residence,* New Jersey
            Jeremiah Ford III, Architect
            Princeton, N.J.

133   *Penque Residence,* Kutztown, Pa.
            Vincent Kling, Architect
            Philadelphia, Pa.

134   *Residence,* Connecticut
            Tim Prentice, Architect
            Norfolk, Conn.

135, 136   *Dent Residence,* Long Island, N.Y.
            Barbara and Julian Neski, Neski Associates
            New York, N.Y.

137   *Pool House/Studio,* East Hampton, N.Y.
            Donald Ritchey, Architect

138   *Residence,* Connecticut
            Philip Johnson
            New York, N.Y.

139   *Residence,* Illinois
            Edward H. Bennett, Jr., Architect
            Chicago, Ill.

140   *Yektai Residence/Studio,* Bridgehampton, N.Y.
            Richard Kaplan, Architect
            New York, N.Y.

141   *Residence,* Long Island, N.Y.
            Richard Kaplan, Architect
            New York, N.Y.

142, 143   *Residence,* Ithaca, N.Y.
            Schickel Development Co.
            Ithaca, N.Y.
            Collaborating Architect:
            Peacock Garn & Partners, Architects
            Cincinnati, Ohio

144   *Residence,* Yorktown Heights, N.Y.
            Robert Felson, Architect
            White Plains, N.Y.

145, 146   *Residence,* Cornwall, Conn.
            Prentice & Chan, Ohlhausen, Architects
            New York, N.Y.

147, 148   *Rosenblatt Residence,* West Hebron, N.Y.
            Charles Mount, Architect
            New York, N.Y.

149   *Residence,* Virginia
            Wilkes & Faulkner Associates
            Washington, D.C.

152, 153   *Residence,* Hudson Valley, N.Y.
            Tom Platt, Architect

154, 155   *Residence,* Bedford, N.Y.
            Myron Henry Goldfinger, Architect
            New York, N.Y.

156, 157   *Residence,* Greenwich, Conn.
            Gwathmey, Siegel Architects
            New York, N.Y.

158, 159   *Residence,* Connecticut
            Hardy Holzman Pfeiffer Associates
            New York, N.Y.

160, 161   *Residence,* Wisconsin
            Stanley Tigerman and Associates, Ltd.
            Chicago, Ill.

162-165   *Christiansen Residence,* Wisconsin
            Stanley Tigerman and Associates, Ltd.
            Chicago, Ill.

168-171   *Barn Homes*
            Dominique Storm van Leeuwen
            Woodstock, N.Y.

172   *Residences,* Sagaponac, N.Y.
            Eugene Futterman, Architect
            Sag Harbor, N.Y.

173 (top)   *Residence*
            Markisz & Magnani
            New York, N.Y.

173 (bottom) *Residence,* Long Island, N.Y.
            Ed Copeland, Architect
            East Hampton, N.Y.

174, 175   *Brook Hollow Condominium,* Hanover, N.H.
            Day and Ertman, Architects
            Lexington, Mass.

178, 179   *Residence,* Nantucket, Mass.
            Louis Mackall, Architect
            Guilford, Conn.

ILLUSTRATION CREDITS

page no.

Title page	Ernest Burden
1	Gil Amiaga
2, 3	Ernest Burden
4, 5	Courtesy Gladys Haberman: 2, 8–15 B. Sean Hay: 1, 3, 5, 7 Irv Wise: 16
6, 7	Ernest Burden: 7, 8 Courtesy Gladys Haberman: 9, 10, 11 B. Sean Hay: 1–6 Irv Wise: 12
8–17	Ernest Burden
18–19	From *Barn Plans and Outbuildings* (New York: Orange Judd, 1904).
20, 21	Ernest Burden: 2–10 Irv Wise: 1
22	Ernest Burden: 1, 5 Irv Wise: 3–4
23–25	Ernest Burden
26–27	From *Old Engravings and Illustrations*. Vol. 2: *Things* (Minneapolis: Dick Sutphen Studio, 1965).
28–41	Ernest Burden
42, 43	Ernest Burden: 4–7 Dominique Storm van Leeuwen: 1–3
44, 45	Peter Beard
46, 47	Courtesy Richard Babcock
48, 49	Courtesy Juster Pope Associates
50	Madra N. Britt
51	Jack Shelton
52	Courtesy Feldhausen Associates
53	Peter Hoftyzer
54	Gil Amiaga
55	Tim Stoenner for Juster Pope Associates
56, 57	Howard A. Patterson, Jr.
58–71	Ernest Burden, except watercolor by Brian Burr: 21
72, 72	Byron Bell: 1, 2, 4 Ernest Burden: 3, 5, 6
74–75	Courtesy Paul Londe
76	Courtesy Barberton Historical Society
77	Ernest Burden
78, 79	Moritz O. Bergmeyer: 1–5, 7–9 Ellen Shoshkis: 6, 10, 11
80, 81	Jay Reiter
82, 83	Courtesy Sheraton Motor Inn
84	Tom Long and Gary Maule for Land Design/Research Inc.
85 (top)	Tom Long and Gary Maule for Land Design/Research Inc.: 4
85 (bottom)	Lee Harris Pomeroy: 1 Ernest Burden: 2
86, 87	Ernest Burden: 2–4, 6, 7, 9 Courtesy Liebman and Hurwitz, Architects & Planners: 1, 5, 8
88, 89	Courtesy Zion & Breen Associates: 1 Norman McGrath: 2–9
90, 91	Gil Amiaga
92	Courtesy Land Design/Research Inc.
93	Ernest Burden
94, 95	Courtesy Power Authority of the State of New York
96, 97	Norman McGrath
98	James Durrell for Schickel Design & Development Co.
99	Philip A. Turner
100–109	Ernest Burden
110 (top)	Donald Sarstedt: 1–4
110 (bottom)	Ernest Burden: 1, 2
111, 112	William Rolland
113	Ernest Burden
114–115	Courtesy William Weber Kirsch, Architect
116, 117	Carl Reik, California Redwood Association
118, 119	Tim Stoenner for Juster Pope Associates
120, 121	Robert Perron
122	Courtesy Francis Booth: 1 Ernest Burden: 2–6
124, 125	Ernest Burden
126	Ernest Burden: 2 Robert Perron: 1, 3, 4
127	Ernest Burden: 1, 2, 3 center and right, 4 Courtesy Charles Coiro, Architect: 3 left
128–130	Ernest Burden
131	Courtesy Jeremiah Ford III: 1 Ernest Burden: 2, 3, 4
132, 133	Ernest Burden
134	Norman McGrath
135–137	Ernest Burden
138–139	Ezra Stoller © ESTO
140–141	Ernest Burden
142, 143	George Lavris for Schickel Design & Development Co.
144	Gil Amiaga
145–149	Norman McGrath
150–151	Ernest Burden
152, 153	Ezra Stoller © ESTO
154, 155	Norman McGrath
156, 157	David Franzen: 2, 3, 5 Courtesy Gwathmey, Siegel Architects: 1, 4 Norman McGrath: 6, 7
158, 159	Courtesy Hardy Holzman Pfeiffer Associates: 2 Noman McGrath: 1, 3–6
160, 161	Philip A. Turner: 2–5 Courtesy Stanley Tigerman and Associates, Ltd.: 1
162, 163	Courtesy Stanley Tigerman and Associates, Ltd.
164, 165	Philip A. Turner
166–167	Courtesy Day and Ertman, Architects
168, 169	Ernest Burden: 1, 11 Courtesy Barn Homes Ltd: 2–10, 12
170, 171	Courtesy Barn Homes Ltd.
172	Ernest Burden: 1, 3, 6 Courtesy Eugene Futterman: 2, 4, 5
173	Gil Amiaga: 7, 8
174, 175	Phokian Karas: 5, 6 Courtesy Day and Ertman, Architects: 1–4
176, 177	Ernest Burden: 1, 2, 4 Irv Wise: 3
178–179	Robert Perron

Index

Art Barn (Greenwich), 93

Babcock, Richard, 46, 47, 104, 105
Baker, James, 90, 91
Barber, Ohio C., 76
Barberton Historical Society, 76
Barn Homes, 70, 71, 168–171
Beadle, Gina, 110
Beard, Peter, 44, 45
Bell, James Byron, 72, 73
Bennett, Edward H., Jr., 139
Benton, Lou and Patricia, 104
Bergmeyer, Moritz, 78, 79
Blenheim-Gilboa Pumped Storage Power
   Project, 94, 95
Bomser, Alan and Jill, 152, 153
Booth, Francis, 122–124
Breen, Harold, 88
Britt, Bill, 50
Brook Hollow, 174, 175
Burr, Brian, 66, 67
Burden, Ernest, 60–69

Callahan, William, 110
Chain O'Lakes Covenant Church, 99
Christiansen, Jim, 162–165
Cobb, Henry Ives, 139
Coiro, Charles, 127, 128
Copeland, Ed, 172
Cullins, Tom and Kelly, 120, 121

Darrow School, 90, 91
Day and Ertman, 174, 175
Dean, Anna, Farm, 76
Dent, Edward, 135, 136

Edelman, Arthur, 127, 128
Elliott, Clinton and Varney, 104

Farmers' Museum, 77
Felson, Robert, 144
Fieldhouse, Homer, 52
Frog Hollow, 162–165
Futterman, Eugene, 172, 173

Ganahl Dairy Barn, 80, 81
George, Phil, 125
Glasser, David, 54

Goldfinger, Myron, 154, 155
Grailville Oratory, 98
Gwathmey, Charles, 156, 157

Hancock Shaker Village, 77
Hardy Holzman Pfeiffer, 96, 97, 158, 159
Heimann, Richard, 109, 113
Hofmann, Natalia, 106–108
Hoftyzer, Peter, 53

Jackson, Peter, 126
Johnson, Philip, 138
Juster Pope Associates, 55, 118

Kaplan, Richard, 140, 141
Kirsch, William, 116, 117
Kittamaqundi Community, 84
Kling, Vincent, 133
Kupper, Tom, 93, 129

Lang, Neil, 84, 92
Lansing Manor, 94, 95
Lattizzori, Richard and Charlotte, 105,
   106
Levitt Residential Communities, 174, 175
Lewis, George, 90, 91
Liebman and Hurwitz, 86, 87
Londe, Paul, 80, 81

Mackall, Louis, 178, 179
Markisz & Magnani, 172
Mason, Susanne, 109
Maryland National Capitol Parks and
   Planning Commission, 92
Montpelier Manor, 92
Mount, Charles, 147, 148

Neski, Julian and Barbara, 135, 136

Orr, Frank, 51

Patterson, Howard, 56, 57
Penque, Ronald, 133
Platt, Tom, 152, 153
Pomeroy, Lee Harris, 85
Prentice, Tim, 134, 145, 146

Ritchey, Donald, 137
Rolland, William, 111, 112

Rosenblatt, Daniel, 147, 148
Rowe, Abplanalp & Johnson, 99
Roxbury Run, 176, 177

Salter, Richard, 88, 89
Sarstedt, Donald, 110
Schickel, William, 98, 142, 143
Schoharie County Historical Society, 94,
   95
Schutz, Herbert D., 129
Scribner Hollow, 176, 177
Sea Ranch, 176, 177
Sheraton Motor Inn (Fredericksburg), 82,
   83
Short & Ford, 131, 132
Simon's Rock Art Center, 96
Sinnott, Edward, & Son, 82, 83
Slater, Milton and Frances, 104
Sloane, Eric, 111, 112
Sloane, Eric, Museum, 77
Stern, Richard and Dorothy, 105
Storm van Leeuwen, Dominique, 70, 71,
   168–171

Tigerman, Stanley, 160, 161, 162–165
Thomson, William M., 130

Warns, Carl, 137
Wilkes & Faulkner Associates, 149
Williams, Arthur, 138
Willmot, Dennis, 120, 121, 126
Wyner, Ed and Muriel, 105, 106

Yektai, Manoucher, 140

Zion, Robert, 88, 89
Zion & Breen, 88, 89